Report It in Writing

FIFTH EDITION

Report It in Writing

DEBBIE J. GOODMAN, M.S.

Miami Dade College
School of Justice
North Campus
Miami, Florida

Prentice Hall

Boston Columbus Indianapolis New York San Francisco Upper Saddle River Amsterdam
Cape Town Dubai London Madrid Milan Munich Paris Montreal Toronto Delhi
Mexico City São Paulo Sydney Hong Kong Seoul Singapore Taipei Tokyo

Editor in Chief: Vernon Anthony
Acquisition Editor: Tim Peyton
Editorial Assistant: Lynda Cramer
Media Project Manager: Karen Bretz
Director of Marketing: David Gesell
Marketing Manager: Adam Kloza
Senior Marketing Coordinator: Alicia Wozniak
Marketing Assistant: Les Roberts
Project Manager: Holly Shufeldt
Creative Director: Jayne Conte
Cover Designer: Axell Designs
Cover Photo: SuperStock
Manager, Cover Visual Research & Permissions: Karen Sanatar
Full-Service: Aparna Yellai, GGS Higher Education Resources,
   A division of Premedia Global, Inc.
Printer/Binder: Edwards Brothers Malloy

Pearson Education LTD.
Pearson Education Australia PTY, Limited
Pearson Education Singapore, Pte. Ltd
Pearson Education North Asia Ltd
Pearson Education, Canada, Ltd
Pearson Educación de Mexico, S.A. de C.V.
Pearson Education–Japan
Pearson Education Malaysia, Pte. Ltd

Library of Congress Cataloging-in-Publication Data

Goodman, Debbie J.
   Report it in writing/Debbie J. Goodman.—5th ed.
      p. cm.
   Includes bibliographical references and index.
   ISBN-13: 978-0-13-609355-8
   ISBN-10: 0-13-609355-8
   1. Police reports.   2. Report writing.
   3. Report writing—Problems, exercises, etc.
   4. English language—Rhetoric.   I. Title.
   HV7936.R53G66 2011
   808'.066363—dc22

                                 2009040536

Prentice Hall
is an imprint of

www.pearsonhighered.com

11 10 9
ISBN-13: 978-0-13-609355-8
ISBN-10: 0-13-609355-8

The Report It in Writing workbook is dedicated to the five greatest people I know: Glenn Goodman, my husband; Connor and Carson Goodman, my sons; and Sunny and Sy Howard, my parents. Glenn, Connor, Carson, Mom, and Dad, thank you for giving me extraordinary happiness. I will always love, respect, and admire you.

To Corinne and Sam: Thank you for your love, kindness, and guidance.

To the men and women of law enforcement and corrections: Thank you for your exceptional service to our communities. May you lead long, happy, and fulfilling lives.

Contents

Preface

The *Report It in Writing* workbook, fifth edition, is now better than ever! Whether you are a trainee, officer, supervisor, or college student, you will find this workbook helpful in your quest to write quality reports. It contains

1. New spelling exercises
2. New punctuation exercises
3. New grammar exercises
4. New proofreading exercises
5. New chronological order exercises
6. New pre- and posttests

All criminal justice professionals know that the ability to write well is an absolutely necessary skill in today's society. A well-written report demonstrates your knowledge and professionalism. A poorly written report could demonstrate laziness and a lack of determination.

In the fifth edition of this popular workbook used by thousands of professionals throughout the country, you will find expanded or new sections on the following topics:

investigative reporting	A–Z guide to report writing
ethical reporting	good listening skills
observation and description	interpersonal communication
establishing rapport	ethics scenarios

and much more!

In addition, both the pretest and the posttest have been expanded to 100 questions each. These are excellent tools to assess your skills at the start and end of your training program. Enjoy the new and improved version of the *Report It in Writing* workbook. Thank you for your service to our communities.

Best wishes,

Debbie J. Goodman, M.S.

Acknowledgments

I would like to acknowledge the following administrators, faculty, and staff of Miami Dade College and the School of Justice in Miami, Florida, for their invaluable support:

Dr. Eduardo Padron, District President
Dr. José Vicente, North Campus President
Ron Grimming, School of Justice Director
Tom Hood, Basic Training Director
Dr. Donna Jennings, Assessment Center Director
Larry LaClair, Security Program Manager
Mary Greene, Business Manager
Sgt. Bucky Greene
Prof. Anna Leggett
Prof. R. Scott Davis
Prof. Ed Hargis
Prof. Mike Grimes
Prof. Fred Hutchings
Prof. Sam Latimore
Prof. Miriam Lorenzo
Prof. Clyde Pfleegor
Prof. Clark Zen
Sgt. Michele Williams
Jean Doubles
Sheila Foster
Regina Seidentopf
Lisa Lavins
Training Supervisors
Training Advisors

To my students, former, present, and future:
Thank you for your commitment to the learning process.

Introduction

Congratulations! By reading this workbook, you have taken the first step toward improving your writing ability. I assure you that the *Report It in Writing* program will be invigorating and that you will see immediate results. I consider the *Report It in Writing* program a mental workout for the dedicated professional. With this workout, you are not required to join a fancy club located miles away from home. With this workout, you are not asked to pay outrageous membership dues. With this workout, you will not feel intimidated.

By using the *Report It in Writing* program as your guide, *you will* watch yourself become a more effective communicator. *You will* use the step-by-step exercises offered in this workbook, to transform your written work into something of which you can be proud.

Many individuals suffer from "uncertainty" when it comes to putting ideas on paper. Some tend to think that the inability to write effectively is something from which they can hide. These individuals eventually realize that the deceptive mask that they have been wearing for so long must be removed one day. When the mask is removed, what will we find? We will find a brave person who is in need of **change**. This six-letter word, *change*, is frightening. However, you will probably agree that continuing along a path of uncertainty is more frightening than embracing the opportunity to improve the quality of your written work.

To achieve a successful workout, you need the following: a burning desire to write well, a willingness to improve your present skill level, and a commitment to your personal pursuit of excellence.

Enjoy the *Report It in Writing* program, and enjoy the newfound confidence that you will ultimately experience. You deserve it!

TOP TWELVE REASONS WHY YOU SHOULD WRITE WELL

1. You are a professional.
2. Professionals are expected to write well.
3. You represent a prominent department.
4. Well-written reports lead to solid convictions of defendants.
5. Well-written reports are used for promotional consideration.
6. Well-written reports help investigations.
7. Well-written reports reflect efficiency and knowledge.
8. You will most likely write each day during your career.
9. Reports are public records.
10. You will gain respect from supervisors, colleagues, and citizens by writing well.
11. Your writing represents not only you but also your department.
12. You'll feel better about yourself knowing that you write well.

Report It in Writing

Pretest

Directions: On the blank provided, write the letter of the under-lined word or phrase that identifies the subject of each sentence.

~~C~~ A 1. The <u>officer</u> <u>transported</u>^{(a) (b)} the <u>suspect</u>^(c) to the <u>station</u>^(d).

A 2. The <u>commander</u>^(a) <u>complimented</u>^(b) <u>Ferguson</u>^(c) during <u>roll call</u>^(d).

~~B~~ A 3. <u>Fingerprints</u>^(a), which belonged to the <u>suspect</u>^(b), were <u>found</u>^(c) on the <u>wall</u>^(d).

A 4. <u>Officer Wilson</u>^(a) made a <u>lawful stop</u>^(b), found <u>cocaine</u>^(c) on the front seat, and arrested the <u>juveniles</u>^(d).

B 5. Prior to the <u>arrest</u>^(a), <u>Officer Jackson</u>^(b) <u>informed</u>^(c) <u>Barnes and Walters</u>^(d) that they had the right to remain silent.

Directions: On the blank provided, place an A if the sentence is written in the active voice or a B if the sentence is written in the passive voice.

B 6. The ticket was written by Officer Adams.

A 7. Officer Blum wrote the ticket.

A 8. I will write a memo to the chief regarding the Specialized Task Force.

B 9. It was determined by the witness that the suspect was a white male.

B 10. At the last minute, an emergency meeting was called by the sergeant.

Directions: On the blank provided before the number, write the letter that identifies the correctly spelled word in each sentence.

_____ B C 11. The _____ searched the inmate's cell for contraband.
a. corpral   b. corporel   c. corporal

_____ B A 12. The armed robbery _____ at 11:00 A.M.
a. occurred   b. occured   c. ocurred

_____ C 13. This crime scene is _____ to last week's scene.
a. similer   b. similiar   c. similar

_____ A 14. I _____ the area and spotted the juvenile.
a. patrolled   b. patroled   c. pattroled

_____ C 15. _____ I will be honored at the graduation.
a. Tomorow   b. Tommorrow   c. Tomorrow

Directions: On the blank provided before the number, write the letter that identifies the correct form of the verb in each sentence.

_____ B A 16. According to officials, the knife, but not the handguns, _____ found.
a. was   b. were

_____ B 17. One of the detectives _____ a vacation.
a. need   b. needs

_____ A 18. Each of the officers _____ mastered writing skills.
a. has   b. have

_____ A 19. The jury _____ reached a guilty verdict.
a. has   b. have

_____ B A 20. Either of the captains _____ ready to retire.
a. is   b. are

Directions: On the blank provided, identify each of the following with an A for a complete sentence or a B for an incomplete sentence.

_____ B 21. Since you understand the material and make every effort to do well and improve.

_____ A 22. The detectives gathered evidence this morning.

_____ B 23. Because he was dazed from being robbed at gunpoint and beaten with a metal pipe.

_____ A 24. If you listen, read, study, and learn, you should graduate from the academy.

_____ A B 25. Although communication skills, both verbal and written, are important.

Directions: On the blank provided before the number, write the letter that identifies the correct word in each sentence.

_____ A B _____ 26. When officers arrest suspects, they must _____ the appropriate statute.
   a. site   b. cite   c. sight

_____ B _____ 27. The correctional officer overheard _____ plan to escape from jail.
   a. they're   b. their   c. there

_____ A B _____ 28. The fight was _____ four males who were all under the age of eighteen.
   a. between   b. among

_____ A _____ 29. _____ Officer Johnson, who else is being honored at the annual police banquet?
   a. Besides   b. Beside

_____ A _____ 30. The victim gave her _____ at the state attorney's office.
   a. deposition   b. disposition

_____ B C _____ 31. The prosecutor wondered whether the drug addict's testimony would be _____.
   a. credential   b. creditable   c. credible

_____ A _____ 32. Morrison _____ her right to an attorney and told Officer Smith everything about the murder.
   a. waived   b. waved

_____ A _____ 33. In order to relieve stress, Officer Byron _____ to exercise in the evening.
   a. chooses   b. choses

_____ B _____ 34. Before entering the cell, the convicted drug dealer _____ off his clothes.
   a. striped   b. stripped

_____ C B _____ 35. _____ under arrest!
   a. You   b. You're   c. Your

Directions: On the blank provided, write A if the sentence demonstrates the correct usage of the semicolon or colon or B if the usage is incorrect.

_____ A _____ 36. The suspect started to run toward the bushes; however, the officer was able to apprehend him.

_____ B _____ 37. The captain said; "Everyone must report to the meeting by noon."

_____ A _____ 38. A police narrative should contain the following elements: who, what, when, where, why, and how.

_____ B A _____ 39. Major Ramirez: Thank you for speaking with the students.

_____ B _____ 40. During the months of November and December; shoplifting episodes start to increase.

Directions: On the blank provided, write A if the sentence demonstrates the correct usage of the comma or B if the usage is incorrect.

_____ B _____ 41. Officer Jamison an avid football fan, attends every Dolphins' home game.

_____ A _____ 42. The police department's supply closet contains pens, pencils, and paper.

_____ B A _____ 43. Officer Williams, an intelligent, professional woman, is highly respected by her colleagues.

_____ A B _____ 44. According to the National Institute of Justice "Juvenile crime, is on the rise."

_____ A _____ 45. Having successfully passed the promotional test, Officer Hernandez celebrated with his family and friends.

Directions: Each sentence contains one mistake. Read each sentence *carefully*. On the blank provided, identify the error by its letter as follows: A (grammar), B (spelling), C (capitalization), or D (punctuation).

_____ C _____ 46. On friday, January 1, 1993, Officer Callahan submitted his memorandum for a salary increase.

_____ B _____ 47. Late last week, Officer Jackson accepted a promotion for her outstanding display of leadership, proffesionalism, and dedication.

_____ B _____ 48. Do you know why Leiutenant Quinn is moving to London, England?

_____ A _____ 49. The chief had to choose between her and myself.

_____ A _____ 50. Who did the victim identify in the lineup?

Directions: On the blank provided, place an A if the sentence is written in the first person or a B if the sentence is written in the third person.

_____ B _____ 51. This unit arrived at the above location at 0900 hours.

_____ A _____ 52. I arrived at the above location at 0900 hours.

_____ A _____ 53. I questioned the juvenile about the incident.

_____ B _____ 54. This reporter questioned the juvenile about the incident.

_____ B _____ 55. This officer saw the inmate fleeing north.

_____ A _____ 56. I saw the inmate fleeing north.

_____ A _____ 57. I heard an inmate scream for help.

_____ B _____ 58. This officer heard an inmate scream for help.

_____ B _____ 59. This unit watched the cell for ten minutes.

_____ A _____ 60. I watched the cell for ten minutes.

Directions: On the blank provided, place an A if the sentence is written in the active voice or a B if it is written in the passive voice.

_____ B _____ 61. The suspect was detained by Officer Nelson.

_____ A _____ 62. I gave the handbook to the inmate.

_____ B _____ 63. Identification was left by the robber.

_____ B _____ 64. The scene was secured by Officer Ramos.

_____ A _____ 65. I transported the suspect.

_____ B _____ 66. The witness was questioned by Officer Johnson.

_____ B _____ 67. A chain-link fence was hit by the vehicle.

_____ A _____ 68. The sergeants gathered the evidence.

_____ B _____ 69. The officer was kicked in the abdomen by the inmate.

_____ B _____ 70. Witnesses were interviewed.

Directions: On the blank provided, identify the punctuation as A (correct) or B (incorrect).

_____ B A _____ 71. When I arrived at the location, I saw a juvenile wearing a black shirt, blue jeans, and sneakers.

_____ B A _____ 72. Sergeant Dixon: I would like to meet with you to discuss the gang-prevention project.

_____ A B _____ 73. The victim yelled, "Help me! Hes going to kill me!"

_____ B _____ 74. The inmate complained of chest pains, therefore I escorted him to the clinic.

_____ A _____ 75. I seized his license and registration.

_____ A B _____ 76. The following officers have been promoted: James Johnson Lucy Reynolds and Steve McGriff.

_____A_____ 77. When I was placing handcuffs on the suspect, he said, "I didn't do it."

_____A B_____ 78. The defendant stole five cassettes from the store I arrested him for retail theft.

_____B_____ 79. The juveniles committed the robbery, therefore; they will be incarcerated.

_____A B_____ 80. I saw a visitor fall down a flight of stairs I immediately called fire rescue.

Directions: On the blank provided before the number, write the letter of the correctly spelled word in each sentence.

_____A_____ 81. The investigator found the _____.
a. bodies   b. bodys

_____B_____ 82. The rapist victimized elderly _____.
a. ladys   b. ladies

_____B_____ 83. The officers seized two _____ from the inmate's cell.
a. knifes   b. knives

_____B_____ 84. The witness saw the suspect _____ down the street.
a. runing   b. running

_____A_____ 85. The officers are _____ a surprise party for Sergeant Greene.
a. planning   b. planing

_____A_____ 86. Officer Brown _____ the area at 0700 hours.
a. patrolled   b. patroled

_____A_____ 87. The defendant said he _____ the murder.
a. committed   b. commited

_____A B_____ 88. The incident _____ at 2300 hours.
a. occured   b. occurred

_____A_____ 89. I _____ appreciate your service to the community.
a. sincerely   b. sincerly

_____B_____ 90. There should be zero tolerance for _____ conduct.
a. legal   b. illegal

Directions: On the blank provided, place an A if the sentence is written in active voice or a B if the sentence is written in passive voice.

_____A_____ 91. Officer Reed searched the vehicle.

_____B_____ 92. The vehicle was searched by Officer Reed.

_____A_____ 93. The officer wrote the report.

_____B_____ 94. The report was written by the officer.

_____B_____ 95. Information about the incident was provided by the victim.

_____A_____ 96. The victim provided information about the incident.

_____B_____ 97. The subject was transported to the station.

_____A_____ 98. I transported the subject to the station.

_____B_____ 99. Fire Rescue #27 was called to the scene.

_____A_____ 100. I called Fire Rescue #27 to the scene.

Score = (# correct × 1) = _____78_____%

SECTION I

The A–Z's of Report Writing

PART A

Report-Writing Rules

Rule 1. Write your narratives in chronological (arranged in time) order. There are three key steps to chronology:

  a. introduction
  b. middle
  c. conclusion

a. The *introduction* is the part of the narrative that establishes why you are on the scene.

Example: At approximately 0900 hours, I was patrolling B Wing when I saw two white male inmates wrestling on the ground. They were punching and kicking each other.

b. The *middle* (also known as the *body*) of the narrative should answer the following key questions: who did what to whom, how, when, where, and why?

Example: When I saw Inmates Frank Lopez and Dave Brock wrestling on the floor of cell P6B1, I immediately radioed for assistance. Officer Scott Carter arrived at my location at approximately 0905 hours. We separated Inmates Lopez and Brock, and we escorted them to a nontrusty dormitory (cell P5C2).

c. The *conclusion* represents your final action(s) as the reporting officer.

Example: At approximately 0915 hours, I informed Shift Commander Rick Jackson of the incident. I took no further action.

Rule 2. Reports must contain specific facts about specific events. A *fact* is something that occurred. A fact can be proven.

An *opinion*, however, is someone's belief. An opinion is open to interpretation. Allow the judge or jury to reach opinions. Stick to the facts, sir! Stick to the facts, ma'am!

Examples:	**Opinion:**	The juvenile was hostile.
	Fact:	The juvenile said, "Kiss off, Cop!"
	Opinion:	The defendant appeared drunk.
	Fact:	The defendant had bloodshot eyes and slurred speech. His breath smelled of an unknown alcoholic beverage.
	Opinion:	The suspect was sarcastic.
	Fact:	When I asked the suspect to touch the tip of his nose, he said, "Why don't you touch it for me?"

Rule 3. Report writers must be as clear as possible when conveying a written message.

Remember that many people read your reports. Each person who reads your narrative must have a clear picture of the incident that took place. Eliminating jargon and slang and writing in natural language will improve the clarity of your writing.

A note on report writing from people in the media is pertinent here. Many times reporters from TV and newspapers read police reports, especially those that are used as evidence in court cases. Nothing is more frustrating to a reporter than a police report that is filled with police jargon. Journalists can't make heads or tails of it, so keep the report free and clear of police lingo. Remember **K.I.S.S.** Keep It Simple, Sir/Ma'am.

Examples:	**Jargon:**	I effected an arrest upon the defendant.
	Natural:	I arrested the defendant.
	Jargon:	We maintained visual surveillance of the suspect for thirty minutes.
	Natural:	We watched the suspect for thirty minutes.
	Jargon:	I telephonically contacted the victim about the incident.
	Natural:	I phoned/called the victim about the incident.

Rule 4. All writers, especially all report writers, should concentrate on writing in a concise (marked by brevity of expression) manner. Of course, some situations require more details than other situations.

You can easily avoid wordiness in your sentences by choosing natural language. Again, to eliminate wordiness, **K.I.S.S.** Be clear and concise with your words.

Examples:	**Wordy:**	The vehicle that the said subject was driving appeared to be new in appearance, and the exterior of the vehicle was brown in color.
	Concise:	The subject was driving a new model brown car.
	Wordy:	I relayed to the juvenile that he was ordered to exit the vehicle, at which time the juvenile alighted from the vehicle; thereby, he complied with my verbal command.
	Concise:	I told the juvenile to get out of the car, and he did.
	Wordy:	I visually perceived that the inmate was in possession of a bag, clear in color, which contained the contents of suspected cocaine.
	Concise:	I saw the inmate holding a clear colored bag, which contained suspected cocaine.

Rule 5. Writers should proofread their reports and memorandums before submitting them to colleagues and supervisors. ***Proofreading*** **is defined as identifying and correcting errors that pertain to the following:**

- Spelling
- Grammar
- Punctuation
- Capitalization
- Sentence structure

Consider these steps to help yourself and others improve their proofreading skills:

R—**R**eview the report for content.
E—**E**valuate the report for errors.
A—**A**nalyze the report for clarity.
D—**D**etermine whether changes need to be made.

Spelling Examples:	Incorrect:	I found drug paraphernellia in the glove compartment of the defendant's car.
	Correct:	I found drug *paraphernalia* in the glove compartment of the defendant's car.
Grammar Examples:	Incorrect:	The investigator questioned he and I.
	Correct:	The investigator questioned *him* and *me*.
Punctuation Examples:	Incorrect:	The inmate was released on parole however he recently committed another crime.
	Correct:	The inmate was released on parole*; however,* he recently committed another crime.
Capitalization Examples:	Incorrect:	I spoke to chief fred reynolds about the case.
	Correct:	I spoke to *Chief Fred Reynolds* about the case.
Sentence Structure Examples:	Incorrect:	I saw a knife with a brown handle entering the cell. (The knife entered?)
	Correct:	When I entered the cell, I saw a knife with a brown handle.

Rule 6. Each and every time you write or critique a report narrative, business letter, or memorandum, review the following lists.

FACTS (THE FIVE W'S AND ONE H)	GRAMMAR	SPELLING
☐ Who	☐ Active Voice	☐ Correct
☐ What	☐ Past Tense	☐ Appropriate Usage
☐ When	☐ Use of I and Me	
☐ Where	☐ No Jargon	
☐ Why	☐ No Slang	
☐ How	☐ Sentence Structure	
	☐ Capitalization	

ORGANIZATION	PUNCTUATION
☐ Chronological Order	☐ Comma
☐ Complete	☐ Period
☐ Concise	☐ Quotation Marks
☐ Clear	☐ Question Mark
☐ Brief	☐ Exclamation Mark
☐ Introduction	☐ Apostrophe
☐ Middle	☐ Semicolon
☐ Conclusion	☐ Colon

Rule 7. Write clearly in field notes and reports. Good report-writing skills are a consideration in both an officer's promotability and in his or her ability to present cases that lead to successful prosecution of suspects.

Rule 8. At times, you will use a tape recorder in these ways:

- As a notebook pad
- To record interviews and statements
- To record phone calls

When you use a tape recorder, you should make transcripts of the taped information, and you should treat the tape as evidence; don't erase it or reuse it!

Rule 9. At times, you will be asked to appear in court. Review the following:

- Elements of the offense
- Probable cause for arrest
- Defendant's version of incident
- Confession (if applicable)
- Prior statements and testimony of witnesses
- Reliability of witnesses
- Warrants and affidavits
- Evidence and reports
- Credibility of witnesses
- Courtroom demeanor

Rule 10. Remember to follow these steps when you write reports:

- Collect information at the crime scene, from informants, and from witnesses.
- Take complete notes.
- Organize the information.
- Prepare the report.
- Proofread and evaluate the report.

PART B

Ten Good Questions

Topic 1: Report Writing

Questions and Answers

Good Question 1:   What is the definition of a **report?**

Answer 1:   A permanent written record regarding important facts to be used in the future defines a **report.**

Good Question 2:   How are reports **used?**

Answer 2:   Reports are **used** for statistics, reference material, officers' evaluations, follow-up activities, and investigative leads.

Good Question 3:   Who **reads reports?**

Answer 3:   Officers, supervisors, attorneys, judges, officials, reporters, and citizens typically **read reports.**

Good Question 4:   What are the **basic steps in report writing?**

Answer 4:   *Gather, record, organize, write,* and *evaluate* refer to the **basic steps in report writing.**

Good Question 5:   When is a report considered **factual?**

Answer 5:   When a report contains no opinions, it is considered **factual.**

Good Question 6:   When is a report considered **clear?**

Answer 6:   A report containing straightforward language and only one interpretation is considered **clear.**

Good Question 7:   When is a report considered **concise?**

Answer 7:   When a report has no unnecessary words, it is considered **concise.**

Good Question 8:   When is a report considered **complete?**

Answer 8:   When answers to all basic questions have been addressed, the report is considered **complete.**

Good Question 9:   All officers should write reports in the **first-person**. What is an example of **first-person reporting?**

Answer 9:   "I questioned" instead of "This officer questioned" is an example of **first-person reporting.**

Good Question 10:   What **skills** do officers need to write quality reports?

Answer 10:   All officers should demonstrate these **skills:** knowledge of proper grammar, spelling, punctuation, capitalization, word usage, and sentence structure to write quality reports.

Topic 2:   Taking Statements

Questions and Answers

Good Question 1:   When should an officer obtain a **statement?**

Answer 1:   At a criminal offense and noncriminal incident, an officer should obtain a **statement.**

Good Question 2:   From **whom** should statements be taken?

Answer 2:   Offenders, witnesses, victims, and other officers are individuals from **whom** statements are obtained.

Good Question 3:   What information should be gathered regarding a **suspect's description?**

Answer 3:   Race, sex, age, height, weight, scars, disabilities, and clothing should be included in a **suspect's description.**

Good Question 4:   What information should be gathered regarding a **vehicle's description?**

Answer 4:   Make, model, style, color, tag number, and identifying marks should be included in a **vehicle's description.**

Good Question 5:   What **questions** should be asked at a criminal offense or noncriminal incident?

Answer 5:   Who, what, when, where, why, and how are **questions** asked regarding a criminal offense or noncriminal incident.

Good Question 6:   What type of information should be gathered regarding **property description?**

Answer 6:   Type, characteristics, estimated value, inscriptions, and owner's name are information should be gathered in **property description.**

Good Question 7:   What **basic procedures** should officers follow when taking statements?

Answer 7:   Reviewing notes, evidence, statements, and rights are **basic procedures** to follow when taking statements.

Good Question 8:   What are the **methods** used for obtaining statements?

Answer 8:   **Methods** for obtaining statements include the use of tape recordings, videotapes, and dictation as well as written statements made by officers or by persons being interviewed.

Good Question 9:   Should someone be present when an officer takes a **juvenile's statement?**

Answer 9:   Yes, a parent should be present when an officer takes a **juvenile's statement.**

Good Question 10:   What information should an officer gather regarding a case involving **injuries?**

Answer 10:   When it comes to **injuries,** officers should address the nature, extent, cause, and seriousness of the injury.

Topic 3:   Note-Taking and Reporting Procedures

Questions and Answers

Good Question 1:   What is the definition of **note taking?**

Answer 1:   Making brief notations concerning specific events defines **note taking.**

Good Question 2:   What are the uses of an officer's **notes?**

Answer 2:   An officer's **notes** can be admitted as evidence, used for writing reports, scrutinized by courtroom staff, and reviewed by follow-up investigators.

Good Question 3:   What **types of information** should an officer enter into a notebook?

Answer 3:   Names of relevant parties, date, time, location, and circumstances of the incident are the **types of information** to enter into a notebook.

Good Question 4:   What **procedures** should officers follow when taking notes?

Answer 4:   Using a notebook, writing with an ink pen, writing legibly, recording relevant facts, and checking spelling of names are **procedures** officers should follow when taking notes.

Good Question 5:   What types of **entry** should an officer include in a notebook?

Answer 5:   Routine types of **entry** in a notebook include statements from witnesses and victims as well as observations of incidents.

Good Question 6:   Why do **reporting procedures** exist?

Answer 6:   **Reporting procedures** exist to ensure uniformity of documents, accuracy, and completeness and to eliminate errors.

Good Question 7:   Why should an officer refer to a **source** for reporting procedures?

Answer 7:   Because reporting procedures may vary from state to state, officers should refer to a relevant **source** regarding appropriate procedures.

Good Question 8:   What are the **basic elements** of reporting procedures?

Answer 8:   A description of what information is to be reported, report forms, circumstances, and a collection of facts are the **basic elements** of reporting procedures.

Good Question 9:   Where may **reporting procedures** be found?

Answer 9:   **Reporting procedures** may be found in state statutes, administrative rules, standard operating procedures, and the report form.

Good Question 10:   What are **two characteristics** of **reporting procedures?**

Answer 10:   Each department should have clear and understandable **reporting procedures** that officers should follow.

TEN GOOD QUESTIONS QUIZ

Directions: On the blank provided, identify the letter of the word or phrase that correctly completes the sentence.

_D_ 1. A permanent written record regarding important facts to be used in the future best defines a

    a. procedural guideline   b. statement
    c. case brief   d. report

_B_ 2. Officers, attorneys, judges, citizens, and officials are considered

    a. writers of reports   b. readers of reports
    c. critics of reports   d. advisers of reports

_A_ 3. When a report contains no opinions, it is considered

    a. factual   b. clear
    c. concise   d. passive

_B_ 4. When a report contains straightforward language, it is considered

    a. factual   b. clear
    c. concise   d. passive

_C_ 5. When all answers to basic questions have been addressed, the report is considered

    a. clear   b. concise
    c. complete   d. correct

_B_ 6. "I wrote the report" is an example of

    a. third-person reporting   b. first-person reporting
    c. second-person reporting   d. passive reporting

_B_ 7. Make, model, and style refer to descriptive information regarding

    a. suspects   b. vehicles
    c. weapons   d. properties

_A_ 8. Race, gender, and height refer to descriptive information regarding

    a. suspects   b. officers
    c. weapons   d. vehicles

_D_ 9. Nature, extent, possible cause, and seriousness are facts that best describe

    a. reports   b. burglaries
    c. thefts   d. injuries

_D_ 10. The five W's and one H refer to

    a. who, what, when, where, and why
    b. who, what, when, and where and why
    c. who, what, and when
    d. who, what, when, where, why, and how

Score = (# correct × 10) = __100__ %

PART C

Ethical Reporting

The Importance of Ethics in the Criminal Justice Field

As a future (or present) criminal justice professional, it is critical that you understand and embrace the importance of ethical conduct and behavior.

The criminal justice profession has been likened to a castle: prestigious, prominent, and deserving of respect. It is critical that the inhabitants of the castle—all future and present criminal justice professionals—commit themselves to upholding and enforcing the law and conducting themselves in accordance with appropriate standards of behavior.

Therefore, in the following pages, I provide you important ethical considerations that are crucial to your success in the criminal justice field.

Ethics, by definition, is the study of morals: good vs. bad, right vs. wrong—plain and simple. We're not going to talk about Plato or Aristotle: For our purposes, getting into the history of philosophers, theorists, and ethicists and their views, perceptions, and arguments is not necessary at this time.

What is necessary is that we in the criminal justice profession (or those who seek to enter) recognize right from wrong, practice it, believe it, uphold it, and enforce it.

"Yeah, you're right—but." But what? I hear this often from students, colleagues, officers, and trainees.

I believe that in this noble profession of ours, there should be no excuses, no shortcuts, no turning the other cheek; just do it. Do what is right, moral, just, legal, and appropriate. Those who like to give the "Yeah—but" argument are telling us that they lack the power, control, and discipline upon which the foundation of this profession is based.

Every day criminal justice professionals must exercise power, control, and discipline, on and off duty. How difficult is it to be courteous, pay for your own stuff, tell the truth, do the best job you are capable of doing, and enforce and uphold the laws of the state in which you live? What's the problem? Let's stick with "Yeah!" instead of "Yeah—but."

Ethics is a Choice

OK, so now you're coming around a bit. I don't expect you to see it my way, not yet—not entirely, anyway. Allow me to further attempt to convince you. You realize that as a criminal justice professional, you're in a fish bowl for all to see. People are watching. We love to watch others. Is this voyeurism? It could be. Whatever you call it, it's reality. So let's be real.

If people are watching what you say and do, how do you want to be perceived?

I want to be perceived as a perfessional worker. I want to be able to inneract with people in a possitive way but if it were to come to taking someone down be able to do it in a manner that won't get me in trouble.

How you want and choose to be perceived will ultimately determine what you become. Ethics is a choice; it's not a fancy concept. It's a choice, so if you choose to be ethical, A to Z, soup to nuts, without the "Yeah—buts," then let's talk.

Making an Ethical Decision

Making an ethical decision, whether it is a personal or professional one, is based upon my ABCD formula:

- *Actions*
- *Beliefs*
- *Conduct*
- *Discipline*

Actions

The way you act—the actions you take day to day—will determine results. Exercise is a good example. Eat well, exercise, don't smoke, don't drink (or if you do, only in moderation), and manage stress, and you should be relatively healthy, according to most doctors. Be intelligent, work hard, don't lie, don't cheat, don't steal, and do your best, and you should stay clear of any internal affairs (IA) investigations.

Beliefs

Believe in yourself, your department, your profession, your family, your religion, and your friends. Believe in the laws of the land, the policies and procedures of your department, and the good of the cause. Believe that ours is a noble profession and stand firm on those beliefs. Believe that you can make a positive difference each and every day. Believe that good guys (and gals) prevail and that the bad ones need to be punished.

Conduct

Conduct yourself as if everyone—mom, dad, wife, uncle, chief, son, and God—was watching. How do you want them to see you? Let them see you as an honorable, trustworthy, dedicated employee. Let them be proud of you and your actions, not shamed and embarrassed by them.

Discipline

If you are tempted, enticed, or intrigued by the possible benefits that immediate gratification may bring, you are human. If, however, you are weak of character and unable to resist temptations in your job, get out or reconsider even joining this profession. We're serious. You need to consider an alternate career because this one is not for you. Too many good, decent, honest, and loyal criminal justice professionals across the country put their lives at risk to make communities better, safer places to live.

The Slippery Slope

If you step foot on a slippery slope, do you increase your odds of falling? This is like asking questions such as these: If you drink alcohol, do you increase your odds of becoming an alcoholic? If you gamble, do you increase your odds (no pun intended) of developing out-of-control gambling behavior? If you speed, do you increase your odds of getting into an accident? The answer to all of these questions is a resounding yes!

The slippery slope theory can be applied to any facet of human behavior. It is important to our discussion of ethics to explore four elements of this theory relative to how we conduct ourselves:

■ *Free will*
■ *Involved participation*
■ *Appropriateness*
■ *Consequences*

First, because we live in a free society, we are afforded the opportunity to move and think freely. The following case is a true example of police trainees who found themselves on the slippery slope and slid rapidly downward. After analyzing this scenario, let's look at the four elements of the theory.

Two police trainees, Rick and Dave, were one week shy of graduating from the police academy. They had successfully completed all classroom and practical areas of the training curriculum and were preparing to take the state certification exam. On Saturday evening, at approximately 11:30 P.M., they decided to go to an exotic dance club, which featured ladies disrobing on stage. While at the club, they ordered several alcoholic drinks and were becoming increasingly loud and obnoxious. On two occasions, the manager told them to settle down. On the third occasion, the manager told them to leave, at which time Rick stood up, pushed the manager, and stated, "Shut the hell up, Asshole. We're cops!" The manager asked for an ID. Dave took out a badge and asked, "OK, Shitface. Satisfied?" The manager went to his office and called the police. Shortly thereafter, the police arrived and arrested Rick for battery, intoxication, and impersonating an officer. Dave was arrested for intoxication and impersonating an officer. Their careers in law enforcement were over. Now, using this scenario, let's address the four elements of the slippery slope theory.

Free Will

Question: Did Rick and Dave exercise free will?
Answer: Yes.

Which of the following statements are true?

1. Rick and Dave decided to go to the exotic dance club.
2. Rick and Dave drank several alcoholic beverages.

3. Rick and Dave became loud and obnoxious.
4. Rick pushed the manager.
5. Rick stated that they were cops.
6. Dave showed the manager a badge.
7. Rick and Dave were disrespectful to the manager.

As you review these statements, you will agree that all are true based on the facts of the case. Let's address the second element of the slippery slope theory.

Involved Participation

The slippery slope theory maintains that behaviors may quickly become increasingly worse, depending on the extent to which the participants are involved. In the Rick and Dave case, both parties were involved in the following:

- Drinking alcoholic beverages
- Becoming loud and obnoxious
- Using profanity
- Impersonating an officer

What do you think would have happened if the two trainees had decided to go to the movies or to a football game instead? Chances are pretty good that they would have graduated from the academy, passed the state certification exam, and started their professional careers.

Appropriateness

On a daily basis, each of us must examine the appropriateness of our behavior. An easy way to make this determination is to consider the following three areas:

1. *Status.* A person's status (e.g., position, rank, title, and professional affiliation) should be considered when deciding on places to go, people with whom to associate, and behavior in which to participate.
2. *Time.* Is the time of day a factor for consideration regarding appropriateness? Yes. Different things may happen at 11:30 A.M. vs. 11:30 P.M. Right?
3. *Place.* Is the place a person is planning to go (e.g., a bar, a church, the beach, a casino) an appropriate place given her or his status? That's for you to decide.

Consequences

The fourth element of the slippery slope theory involves consequences. Remember the saying, "Let your conscience be your guide." When you analyze ethics, if the consequences of potential actions appear stringent and potentially damaging to your health, safety, and career, let your conscience be your guide: Refrain. By not stepping onto the slippery slope but taking the high road instead, you are using your most impressive weapon: your brain.

An Ethics Discussion

"Is it OK for an officer to accept free coffee, food, and other stuff?" asked the inquisitive trainee. The answer to this question has been debated for years and will continue to be argued for years to come.

To provide an appropriate response to this often-asked question, we need to analyze the definition of the term *ethics*. Ethics *refers to principles of accepted rules of conduct for a particular individual or group as mandated by law, policy, or procedure.* Let's examine each component of this definition of ethics.

Principles of Accepted Rules of Conduct

Almost everything in life is based on rules. Sports enthusiasts are familiar with the rules of football. When a player is cited for an illegal face mask, he has broken an important rule of the game and will incur a penalty. That penalty may adversely impact him as well as his teammates. At the police academy, a trainee who violates an institutional rule may find himself or herself facing counseling, a reprimand, or stringent disciplinary action. At the police or corrections department, an officer who does not adhere to the rules can encounter unwanted media attention, liability, and even termination. Therefore, it's fair to say that a significant consequence could act as a deterrent for future inappropriate behavior. However, if no consequence exists or if the consequence is not enforced, the rule breaker may be inspired to continue along a path of inappropriate conduct.

Rules for a Particular Individual or Group

Doctors, lawyers, accountants, and police officers have something in common. These professionals must adhere to strict guidelines in order to maintain their certifications. Professionals of this caliber are held to high standards, and each group member has a unique ethical code to which he or she must comply. Failure to comply can result in decertification.

Rules Mandated by Law, Policy, or Procedure

When something is in writing, we notice it, read it, refer to it, remember it, and ultimately *adhere* to it. Therefore, if criminal justice directors, administrators, trainers, practitioners, and educators are serious about *enforcing ethics*, they must work collaboratively to implement specific state (and even federal) guidelines that police and corrections departments must follow. Additionally, department representatives could reinforce these guidelines by writing policies and procedures that explain, clearly and completely, the behaviors that will and will not be tolerated for officers representing their police or corrections department. Criminal justice from professionals at all levels must exhibit these behaviors.

The following illustration easily could be added to a department's standard operating procedures under the ethics category. The following behaviors are unacceptable, and this department views them as unethical:

1. Accepting gratuities (e.g., gifts, favors, money, or anything given to you for free)
2. Using unnecessary force (e.g., physical abuse, emotional mistreatment, or roughing up suspects in custody)
3. Discriminating (mistreating individuals on the basis of race, age, gender, religion, culture, sexual preference, or national origin)
4. Lying in any form (including creating facts to incriminate or protect another)
5. Violating laws, rights, or procedures (e.g., intentionally making a false arrest, filing a false report, or purposely ignoring departmental procedures).

Question: Are you willing to compromise your professional integrity by "overlooking" occurrences that should be documented in writing?

Answer: No! You are an ***ethical officer*** who is called upon to carry out many challenging duties and responsibilities. One critical duty you must perform is reporting any inappropriate incident that takes place. As an officer, you must remain focused on your fundamental mission: to maintain control of the environment and enforce the laws. As a police officer, you must enforce ethics, and if you ***choose*** to overlook an incident by failing to report it, you are doing a grave disservice to your department and to yourself. Failing to document an incident when you should do so could result in joint and several liability. Remember that you are not called upon to be ***friends*** with those with whom you work or supervise. Are you willing to go to jail or prison for a ***friend?***

Ethics Quiz

Directions: Take the following quiz. Discuss your responses with your colleagues.

In the space provided, place an E if you believe the behavior is ethical for officers. Place a U if you believe the behavior is unethical for officers.

_____U_____ 1. Accepting a free meal
_____U_____ 2. Accepting a gift from a citizen
_____U_____ 3. Not ticketing fellow officers
_____U_____ 4. Misusing duty time
_____U_____ 5. Misusing sick time
_____U_____ 6. Speeding
_____U_____ 7. Divulging confidential information
_____U_____ 8. Destroying evidence
_____U_____ 9. Creating incriminating evidence
_____U_____ 10. Using unnecessary force
_____U_____ 11. Offering biased testimony
_____U_____ 12. Lying to protect another officer
_____U_____ 13. Treating people differently on the basis of race, gender, or religion
_____U_____ 14. Making a false arrest
_____U_____ 15. Filing a false report
_____U_____ 16. Reselling confiscated drugs
_____U_____ 17. Acting in a discourteous manner to the public
_____U_____ 18. Misusing patrol vehicles and equipment
_____U_____ 19. Looking the other way when you witness another's unethical conduct
_____U_____ 20. Ignoring departmental policy

Exercise

Review the following ethics scenarios on the following pages from my *Enforcing Ethics* workbook available through Prentice Hall (www.prenhall.com or 1-800-526-0485). Think critically and carefully about your answers. Many criminal justice agencies are asking future employees to respond to ethics-related questions and scenarios as part of the interview process. Also, for those presently working in the field, ethics scenarios are becoming an increasingly popular tool for promotional exams. Good luck!

Ethical Reporting Scenarios

Scenario 1

ETHICAL REPORTING SCENARIO

This is your first week on the job as a police officer. You learned much at the academy, and now you are ready to fight crime and make a difference in society. The dispatcher informed you of your first domestic violence call. You arrived to find that the defendant is a fellow officer from your academy class. The victim, his wife, tells you he punched her in the lip.

Ethically, what should you do?

I would observe the wife to see if their was any bruises to her face like she stated. Then I would arrest the husband and take the victim's statement and then the husbands statement to see if it was in self-defence. If it were to come off as self-defence I would see what we could work out to make sure that this doesn't happen again.

Call a supervisior

Scenario 2

ETHICAL REPORTING SCENARIO

You are a corrections officer who responds to Cell Block B to find Inmates Jones and Martin fighting on the ground. You break them up and separate them. Inmate Martin tells you, "If you know what's good for you, guard, you ain't gonna write this up."

Ethically, what should you do?

Ethically I would question the inmate if he was threatning me. If he were to respond with yes I would let it go and write up a report about the fight and the threat the inmate possed on me.

Scenario 3

ETHICAL REPORTING SCENARIO

You are a newly promoted sergeant and oversee five officers. During the midnight shift, you decide to patrol the neighborhood to "check up" on the guys. To your surprise, at approximately 1:15 A.M., you find Officer Hudson pulled over under a tree at the park, asleep in his patrol car.

Ethically, what should you do?

I would drive over to wake up the officer to tell him in a perfessional manner to get back to work and be on my way.

Document it!!

Scenario 4

ETHICAL REPORTING SCENARIO

You and your partner respond to a call from an affluent part of town and arrive at an upscale home. A neighbor reported not having seen Mr. Samuels leave his residence in over a week.

You enter Mr. Samuels' residence and find him deceased in the living room. He is wearing a Rolex watch and a gold bracelet. Your partner says, "Oh, well. He won't be needing these anymore," and takes the watch and bracelet and puts them in his pocket.

Ethically, what should you do?

I would tell my partner to put back the watch and bracelet because he just tampered with a crime scene. When I write a report I would tell them about the situation that accord. If the officer didn't put the watch and bratelet back I would arrest him.

Scenario 5

ETHICAL REPORTING SCENARIO

You suspect that one of the officers in your unit, Officer Dixon, has a drinking problem. On more than one occasion, you smelled an alcoholic beverage on his breath and heard him tell other officers about his partying.

Tonight you were dispatched to a burglary in progress. You called for backup, but Officer Dixon did not show up to assist you. You were able to handle the call yourself. When you got back to the station, Officer Dixon came up to you with bloodshot eyes and slurred speech. He said, "Listen, Man, I'm sorry I didn't make the call. Just list us both as the responding officers."

Ethically, what should you do?

Report him to higher up

_____

_____

_____

_____

_____

_____

_____

_____

_____

_____

Scenario 6

ETHICAL REPORTING SCENARIO

This is your first week on the job as a newly sworn police officer. You performed well in all of your classes at the academy. You particularly enjoyed the ethics class. You found the scenarios interesting, and you made a promise to yourself that you would never accept freebies or act in a manner unbecoming to the profession. In fact, your department's policy states that officers are not permitted to accept free or discounted meals. Today, you and two senior officers cleared a lunch break with the dispatcher. You enjoyed a pleasant lunch of a club sandwich. After the meal, your fellow officers got up to leave as you reached for your wallet. One officer asked, "What are you doing?" You responded, "I'm paying for my lunch." He said, "Kid, it's on the house. That's why we eat here." You responded, "At the academy, we were taught accepting discounted or free meals is unethical." Both officers laughed and said, "Kid, forget the academy. This is the real world."

Ethically, what should you do? Would you report the officers?

Pay for my meal

Scenario 7

ETHICAL REPORTING SCENARIO

You and your partner were dispatched to a robbery call. The dispatcher described the suspect as a white male juvenile, approximately fifteen to seventeen years of age, wearing a black T-shirt, blue jeans, and tennis shoes. A few blocks east of the scene, your partner saw someone who fit the suspect's description. Your partner exited the patrol car and shouted, "Police! Stop!" The juvenile started running, and your partner ran after him. Moments later, your partner fired his revolver, shooting the juvenile in the back. You called fire rescue. Rescuer responded and transported the juvenile to the hospital. Meanwhile, your partner took you aside and said, "I need you to back me. You gotta help me. No matter who asks, tell them it looked like the kid was about to draw a weapon." (The truth is that the juvenile did not have a weapon.) Later that day, Officer Thomas from Internal Affairs asked you to tell him what happened.

Ethically, what should you do?

Report everything that happened

Scenario 8

ETHICAL REPORTING SCENARIO

You are a corrections officer who works in a maximum security facility. Yesterday, you misplaced your keys. Fortunately, Inmate Jones found your keys, and he returned them to you. Tonight, he told you he received a letter from his wife, who is filing for divorce. At "lights out," he asked you if he can use the phone to call her. He had already used the phone earlier in the day.

Ethically, what should you do?

Report myself that I lost my keys.

Scenario 9

ETHICAL REPORTING SCENARIO

You are an off-duty officer who completed a three-mile run. You decided to cool off and rest under a big oak tree. You sat down under the tree and saw a brown leather wallet close by. Curiosity got the best of you, and you opened the wallet. You found credit cards, identification, and $300 in cash. Nobody else is around.

Ethically, what should you do? What if you had found $3,000, $30,000, or more?

find the person that lost the wallet or take it into the police department.

Scenario 10

ETHICAL REPORTING SCENARIO

You are a probationary police officer. In two weeks, you will be on permanent status with your department. You have heard your immediate supervisor, Sergeant Richards, repeatedly make inappropriate comments to your colleague, a female probationary police officer regarding her "beautiful face" and "knock-out figure." This morning, you overheard Sergeant Richards tell her, "If you don't go out with me, you'll never make it past your probationary stage." She decided to file a report.

Ethically, what should you do? Will you report what you heard?

Report it

Again, if you would like to explore the topic of ethics further, you may want to read my book *Enforcing Ethics*. It is available from Prentice Hall Publishing (1-800-526-0485) or www.prenhall.com.

PART D

Chronological Order

Rule to Remember

Writers of reports should always record events as they occur in chronological order. *Webster's Dictionary* defines *chronology* as "determining events and sequences according to time."

Your report will read well if events and ideas are written in a clear and organized manner.

The following ten actions are listed out of order:

1. I arrested the suspect.
2. The suspect resisted arrest.
3. I stopped the suspect who fit the BOLO description.
4. I questioned the suspect about an armed robbery.
5. I conducted a pat-down search of the suspect and retrieved a 35-caliber revolver from the suspect's right pocket.
6. I received a call from the dispatcher regarding an armed robbery.
7. I grabbed the suspect by the shoulder to stop his movement.
8. I read the suspect the Miranda warnings from my card.
9. The dispatcher described the suspect as a white male, approximately twenty to twenty-three years of age, wearing a red baseball cap and blue jeans.
10. The suspect started to run away from me.

Exercise 1

Directions: Read each sentence on page 42 carefully. Determine the chronological order of each sentence and write it in. (There may be several different correct answers.)

1. _6_____6_____

2. _9_____9_____

3. _3_____3_____

4. _4_____5_____

5. _10_____4_____

6. _7_____10_____

7. _5_____7_____

8. _2_____2_____

9. _1_____1_____

10. _2_____8_____

Exercise 2

Directions: Place an A, B, or C by the chronological sequence of events in the following exercise for first, second, or third, respectively.

___C___ 1. I told Nettles to step out of the car.

___A___ 2. While patrolling the downtown area, I saw Nettles fail to stop at a red light.

___B___ 3. I asked the dispatcher to check the tag (LTM 489), and she told me the car was stolen.

Exercise 3

Directions: Place an A, B, or C by the chronological sequence of events in the following exercise for first, second, or third, respectively.

_C_____ 1. At 6:20 P.M., Smith and I discovered the body.

_B_____ 2. At 6:18 P.M., Smith and I entered the house.

_A_____ 3. I arrived at 6:15 P.M. when I saw Smith standing at the corner of third and Main Street.

Exercise 4

Directions: Place an A, B, or C by the chronological sequence of events in the following exercise for first, second, or third, respectively.

_B_____ 1. The dispatcher described the suspect as follows: white female, approximately fifteen to seventeen years old, wearing a red T-shirt and white shorts.

_A_____ 2. I received a call about a female suspect.

_C_____ 3. I stopped the suspect who fit the BOLO description.

Exercise 5

Directions: Place an A, B, or C by the chronological sequence of events in the following exercise for first, second, or third, respectively.

_C_____ 1. At 0821 hours, Corporal Anderson called for immediate assistance.

_B_____ 2. At 0820 hours, Corporal Anderson walked toward B Wing where he saw five inmates fighting.

_A_____ 3. At 0800 hours, Corporal Anderson arrived on duty.

Exercise 6

Directions: Place an A, B, or C by the chronological sequence of events in the following exercise for first, second, or third, respectively.

_C_____ 1. Officer Farino took the evidence, placed it in an envelope, and submitted it to the laboratory.

_A_____ 2. Officer Farino conducted a pat-down search of Inmate Kelly's clothing.

_B_____ 3. Officer Farino retrieved a suspected marijuana cigarette from Inmate Kelly's right pants pocket.

Exercise 7

Directions: Place an A, B, or C by the chronological sequence of events in the following exercise for first, second, or third, respectively.

_____C_____ 1. You asked the defendant for her driver's license.

_____B_____ 2. You stopped the defendant at the corner of the block.

_____A_____ 3. You saw the defendant weave in and out of traffic.

PART E

Fact vs. Opinion

Rule to Remember

Reports must contain specific *facts* about specific events. A *fact* is something that occurred and a *fact* can be proven.

An *opinion,* however, is someone's belief. An opinion is open to interpretation. Allow the judge or jury to reach opinions. Stick to the facts, sir! Stick to the facts, ma'am!

Examples:

1. **Fact:** A man's body was found near a lake.
   Opinion: The men fishing by the lake probably committed the crime.

2. **Fact:** An eighty-year-old woman called the police.
   Opinion: She is probably lonely, confused, and in need of attention.

3. **Fact:** The juvenile has tattoos on his arm.
   Opinion: He thinks he looks like a tough guy.

4. **Fact:** The officer confiscated twenty-six handguns from the trunk of the defendant's car.
   Opinion: The guns were most likely smuggled in from overseas.

Exercise 1

Directions: Read each sentence carefully. In the space provided, place an F if the sentence expresses a fact or an O if the sentence expresses an opinion.

___F___ 1. The suspect is a sixteen-year-old white male who is wearing green shorts and a yellow shirt.

_O F_ 2. The juvenile has a bad attitude.

___F___ 3. He waived his right to an attorney.

___O___ 4. He probably committed the burglary.

___O___ 5. Her nervous mannerism tells me she knows something about the murder.

___F___ 6. The woman pulled out a knife and stabbed her boyfriend six times in the chest.

___O___ 7. The robber probably stole the jewels from the pawn shop.

___F___ 8. The robbery took place at 0800 hours.

___O___ 9. Whether you think so or not, I am convinced the defendant is guilty.

___F___ 10. The house alarm went off at 2100 hours.

Score = (# correct × 10) = ___90___ %

Exercise 2

Directions: In the space provided, place an F if the sentence expresses a fact or an O if the sentence expresses an opinion.

_O F_ 1. The juvenile was hostile.

_O F_ 2. The suspect was belligerent.

_O F_ 3. The visitor was nervous.

_O F_ 4. The defendant was unusual in appearance.

_O F_ 5. The juvenile was uncooperative.

___O___ 6. He was probably involved in the incident.

_O F_ 7. His conduct was suspicious.

_O F_ 8. Her behavior was out of the ordinary.

___O___ 9. He looked drunk.

_O F_ 10. The inmate was sarcastic.

Score = (# correct × 10) = _____ %

Exercise 3

Directions: In the space provided, place an F if the sentence expresses a fact or an O if the sentence expresses an opinion.

_____F_____ 1. The juvenile said, "Kiss off!"

_____F_____ 2. When I ordered the inmate to step out of the cell, he said, "Screw you, asshole!"

_____F_____ 3. I saw the inmate walking back and forth along the kitchen floor for ten minutes.

_____F_____ 4. I saw the defendant wearing a black trench coat and black ski mask.

_____F_____ 5. The juvenile said, "I don't know shit!"

_____F_____ 6. I found tools (in plain view) in the inmate's cell.

_____F_____ 7. I observed the suspect crouching down behind the bushes.

_____F_____ 8. I heard a female inmate shout, "I'm the savior! I will save the world!"

_____F_____ 9. The suspect had bloodshot eyes and slurred speech. His breath smelled of an unknown alcoholic beverage.

_____F_____ 10. When I asked the suspect to touch the tip of his nose, he said, "Why don't you touch it for me?"

Score = (# correct × 10) = ___10___ %

Exercise 4

Directions: In the space provided, place an F if the sentence expresses a fact or an O if the sentence expresses an opinion.

_____F_____ 1. He was wearing a blue shirt.

_____F_____ 2. The inmate had a tattoo of a cross on his left arm.

_____O_____ 3. The cell appeared dirty.

_____F_____ 4. He punched me in the nose.

_____O_____ 5. The officer looked tired.

_____F_____ 6. The defendant yelled, "Shut up!"

_____F_____ 7. The suspect wore white sneakers.

_____F_____ 8. The inmates were watching television.

_____O_____ 9. She spoke in a nervous tone.

_____F_____ 10. His fists were clenched.

Score = (# correct × 10) = ___100___ %

PART F

Vague vs. Specific Language

Rule to Remember

Eliminate uncertainty! Concentrate on clarity.

When writing a report, leave vague, interpretive language out! Reports must contain specific facts, specific details, and specific (not vague) words. When you write your reports in a clear manner, you feel confident in knowing that you have performed your role in a professional manner and you gain the respect of your colleagues and supervisors. Vague language can also be *wordy*. Specific language is not only clear; it also is *concise*. Who wouldn't want that?

Examples:

1. **Fuzzy:** I <u>verbally articulated</u> to the suspect that he was not free to leave.

   Clear: I <u>told</u> the suspect that he was not free to leave.

2. **Fuzzy:** I <u>effected an arrest upon</u> the defendant.

   Clear: I <u>arrested</u> the defendant.

3. **Fuzzy:** <u>It was reported by the witness</u> that the suspect was a white male.

   Clear: <u>The witness said</u> that the suspect was a white male.

Exercise 1

Directions: The following sentences have vague information. Rewrite each sentence by replacing the underlined word or phrase with specific details.

1. I <u>requested</u> to the driver that he get out of the car.

   I told the driver to get out of the car.

2. I <u>contacted</u> the victim the day after the rape took place.

   I called the victim the day after.

3. The juveniles were involved in a <u>verbal altercation</u>.

   The juveniles were involved in a argument.

4. I have no comment <u>at this present moment in time</u>.

   I have no comment at the time.

5. I arrested the suspect <u>due to the fact that</u> he was carrying a concealed weapon.

   I arrested the suspect for carrying a concealed weapon.

6. <u>It was determined by</u> the witness that the suspect was driving a motorcycle.

   The witness said

7. The assault <u>originated</u> at the corner of Madison Avenue and Walnut Street.

   Started

8. I questioned the suspect <u>in reference</u> to the burglary.

   I questioned the suspect about the burglary.

9. I <u>proceeded to interview</u> the robbery suspect.

   questioned

10. The two juveniles were involved in a <u>physical altercation</u>.

    fight

Score = (# correct × 10) = _____ %

Exercise 2

Directions: Read each sentence carefully. Rewrite the vague sentence using specific details.

1. It was _determined_ that the subject wore a black coat.
   The subject wore a black coat

2. It was _ascertained_ that the watch was stolen.
   It was said the watch was stolen

3. It was _concluded_ that the juveniles committed the robbery.
   It was said the juveniles committed the robb

4. It was _observed_ that the passenger had a gun in his carry-on luggage.
   It was seen that the passenger had a gun in hi carry-on luggage.

5. It was _ascertained_ that the driver smelled of an alcoholic beverage.
   Smelled

6. It was _determined_ that the fingerprint matched the one found at the scene.
   Proven

7. It was _stated_ by the victim that the subject was an Anglo male.
   Said, verified

8. It was _observed_ by the major that the captain arrived at the meeting early.

9. Gas masks were _instructed_ to be put on by the SWAT commander.
   told,

10. It was _requested_ that the chief attend the ceremonial banquet.
    The chief was requested to attend the ceremonial banquet.

Score = (# correct × 10) = _____ %

Exercise 3

Directions: The following sentences have vague information. Rewrite each sentence by replacing the underlined word or phrase with specific details.

1. I noticed the suspect was <u>acting suspicious</u>.

   I noticed a man in black walk around back.

2. The driver of the <u>vehicle was speeding</u>.

   The driver was driving at 90 mph.

3. I found <u>drug paraphernalia</u> in the car.

   I found a bong in the car.

4. I found a <u>weapon</u> in the inmate's cell.

   I found a shank in the inmate's cell.

5. The suspect was <u>acting hostile</u>.

   _____

6. The defendant was <u>obviously drunk</u>.

   The defendant was tripping over his feet.

7. The car was in <u>poor condition</u>.

   The car was dented and smoked.

8. The inmate <u>threatened</u> me.

   The inmate said he was going

9. I seized the <u>evidence</u>.

   I seized 3 pounds of cocaine.

10. I searched the house and found <u>weapons</u>.

    I searched the house and found 7 guns, and 3 knives.

Score = (# correct × 10) = _____%

Exercise 4

Directions: Read each sentence carefully. Rewrite the vague sentence into a clear sentence.

1. Her conduct was suspicious in nature.

   _____

2. His behavior was strange.

   _____

3. The suspect was unusual in appearance.

   _____

4. The defendant was uncooperative.

   _____

5. The juvenile was becoming belligerent.

   _____

6. The landlord appeared angry.

   The landlord was angry.

7. The bank teller was nervous.

   _____

8. The inmate was possessive.

   _____

9. It looked as though the suspect was armed.

   It looked like the suspect was armed.

10. I believed he was under the influence of alcohol.

    I believed he was drunk

Score = (# correct × 10) = _____%

Exercise 5

Directions: In the space provided, choose one of the following clearer terms for the word or phrase in the parentheses.

<table>
<tr><td>saw</td><td>because</td></tr>
<tr><td>called</td><td>started</td></tr>
<tr><td>about</td><td>watched</td></tr>
<tr><td>then</td><td>interviewed</td></tr>
<tr><td>said</td><td>arrested</td></tr>
</table>

1. We (maintained surveillance of) _watched_ the house for twenty-five minutes.

2. I (telephonically contacted) _called_ the victim about the armed robbery.

3. The witness (related) _Said_ the suspect drove a 1990 Toyota Corolla.

4. I (visually observed) _Saw_ the suspect drive his car through a wooden fence.

5. I arrested the suspect for driving under the influence of alcohol (at that present moment in time) _then_.

6. I questioned the witness (due to the fact that) _because_ he said he saw what happened.

7. I (effected an arrest upon) _arrested_ the defendant for carrying a concealed weapon.

8. I questioned the clerk (in reference to) _about_ the drive-by shooting.

9. Investigator Williams (proceeded to conduct an interview with) _interviewed_ the victim.

10. The fight (commenced) _started_ at the corner of Sycamore Avenue and Main Street.

Score = (# correct × 10) = _____ %

Exercise 6

Directions: In the space provided, write the letter of the specific statement in Column II that corresponds with the vague statement in Column I.

COLUMN I

_B_ 1. The juvenile is young.
_A_ 2. I arrived home late.
_D_ 3. The man is heavy.
_G_ 4. The woman is tall.
_E_ 5. I seized the evidence.
_I_ 6. The defendant was speeding.
_C_ 7. The suspect was transported.
_J_ 8. The suspects were Mirandized.
_F_ 9. The witness was questioned.
_H_ 10. The defendant was sentenced.

COLUMN II

A. I arrived home at 1:30 A.M.
B. Ricky is fourteen years old.
C. I drove Hall to the station.
D. Bill weighs 275 pounds.
E. I seized six knives.
F. I questioned Diaz about the arson.
G. Mary is more than six feet tall.
H. Larson was sentenced to life in prison.
I. Taylor was traveling eighty-five miles per hour.
J. I read Smith and Sawyer the Miranda warnings from my card.

Score = (# correct × 10) = _____%

Exercise 7

Directions: Change these "wordy" statements into clear, concise statements.

1. At this present moment in time, I want to relay information to you on the subject of writing in a manner that is free from ambiguous, vague, and unclear language.

   _____

   _____

2. The vehicle that the said defendant was driving was new in appearance, the tires were round in shape, and the exterior of the vehicle was brown in color.

   The defendant was driving a newer
   brown vehicle.

3. I proceeded to conduct an interview with the victim for the purpose of extracting information regarding the physical confrontation, which took place as a result of the fact that the victim looked at the defendant's girlfriend in a presumably negative fashion, which initiated the confrontation.

   _____

   _____

4. I verbally articulated to the defendant that his ability to move freely had been curtailed immediately.

_____

_____

5. I proceeded to make inquiry of the victim regarding the precise whereabouts of the victim's car.

_____

_____

6. I visually perceived that the defendant was in possession of a bag, blue in color, which contained the contents of cocaine.

_____

_____

7. I inquired of the witness on the subject of the direction of travel regarding the suspect.

_____

_____

8. We were given an occasion whereby we were able to meet with the committee representatives to review the upcoming budget for the proposed fiscal year of 2010.

_____

_____

9. I effected an arrest upon the defendant as a result of the fact that he was in the possession of a vehicle that had been stolen.

_____

_____

10. I relayed to the suspect that he was ordered to get out of the car at which time the suspect alighted from the vehicle; thereby, he complied with my request.

_____

_____

Score = (# correct × 10) = _____%

PART G

Common Abbreviations for Note Taking

Rule to Remember

Abbreviations should be used for purposes of note taking; however, most state guidelines do not recommend the use of abbreviations for report writing.

ADW	Assault with a deadly weapon
AKA	Also known as
AMT	Amount
APPROX	Approximately
APT	Apartment
ARR	Arrest
ATT	Attempt or attached
ATTN	Attention
BKG	Booking
BLDG	Building
CAPT; CPT	Captain
CCW	Carrying a concealed weapon
COMDR	Commander
COMP	Complainant
CPL	Corporal
DEFT	Defendant
DEPT	Department
DMV	Department of Motor Vehicles
DNA	Does not apply
DOA	Dead on arrival
DOB	Date of birth
E/B	Eastbound
ETC	And so forth
FED	Federal
FI	Field interview

FTO	Field training officer
GOA	Gone on arrival
HBD	Had been drinking
HGT	Height
HQ	Headquarters
INV	Investigation
JUV	Juvenile
L/F	Left front
LIC	License
LKA	Last known address
L/R	Left rear
LT	Lieutenant
MAJ	Major
N/B	Northbound
NCIC	National Crime Information Center
NFD	No further description
NMI	No middle initial
OFC; OFF	Officer
PC	Penal code or probable cause
POE	Point of entry or point of exit
QTY	Quantity
R/F	Right front
R/O	Reporting officer
R/R	Right rear
RTE	Route
S/B	Southbound
SGT	Sergeant
SUBJ	Subject
SUSP	Suspect
U.S.	United States
VC	Vehicle code
VEH	Vehicle
VICT	Victim
VIN	Vehicle identification number
WAR	Warrant
W/B	Westbound
WIT	Witness

Exercise 1

Directions: On the blank provided, write the appropriate abbreviation for each of the following words or phrases.

Off   1. officer

Sgt   2. sergeant

_lt_   3. lieutenant

Capt   4. captain

CCW   5. carrying a concealed weapon

VIN   6. vehicle identification number

PoE   7. point of entry

Wit   8. witness

Juv   9. juvenile

AKA   10. also known as

Score = (# correct × 10) = _____%

Exercise 2

Directions: On the blank provided, write the appropriate abbreviation for each of the underlined words or phrases.

AKA   1. The gang member is <u>also known as</u> "Sweetie."

Approx   2. The burglary took place at <u>approximately</u> 3:00 P.M.

DOB   3. The subject's <u>date of birth</u> is December 3, 1951.

FTO   4. The perpetrator was running north when the <u>field training officer</u> spotted him.

Vict   5. The <u>victim</u> was shaking and crying from fear.

SGT   6. The <u>sergeant</u> approved your report.

WAR   7. The officer has a signed <u>warrant</u> for your arrest.

MAJ   8. <u>Major</u> Donovan was honored at the annual police banquet.

ADW   9. The teenager has been charged with <u>assault with a deadly weapon</u>.

BLDG   10. The <u>building</u> was evacuated when a tenant smelled smoke.

Score = (# correct × 10) _____%

PART H

Who vs. Whom

Rule to Remember

Who is often used as a subject in a sentence. Replace the word *who* with the word *he, she,* or *they* to check whether you have used the word correctly.

Whom is often used as an object in a sentence. Replace the word *whom* with the word *him, her,* or *them* to check whether you have used the word correctly.

Examples:

Incorrect:	Is this the juvenile <u>whom</u> started the fight?
Correct:	Is this the juvenile <u>who</u> started the fight?

The writer can replace the word *who* with the word *he.* (He started the fight.)

Incorrect:	He is the trainee <u>who</u> I recommend.
Correct:	He is the trainee <u>whom</u> I recommend.

The writer can replace the word *whom* with the word *him.* (I recommend *him.*)

Incorrect:	<u>Whom</u> received the highest score on the exam?
Correct:	<u>Who</u> received the highest score on the exam?

The writer can replace the word *who* with the word *she.* (*She* received the highest score.)

59

Exercise 1

Directions: On the blank provided, write the appropriate word in parentheses in the following sentences.

Who   1. (Who, Whom) do you think killed the victim?

who   2. Do you know (who, whom) is in charge of the Monroe case?

Whom   3. (Who, Whom) did the captain want to interview?

who   4. Is this the inmate (who, whom) started the fight?

Whom   5. Hello. With (who, whom) am I speaking?

Who   6. (Who, Whom) dialed 911?

Who   7. (Who, Whom) got the promotion?

who   8. She is the officer (who, whom) I recommend.

who   9. The inmate (who, whom) was in prison has been released.

Whom   10. (Who, Whom) did the captain appoint as his assistant?

Score = (# correct × 10) = _____%

Exercise 2

Directions: On the blank provided, write the appropriate word in parentheses in the following sentences.

Who   1. The detective (who, whom) investigated the fire solved the case.

Who   2. (Who, Whom) wrote the incident report?

Whom   3. The defendant (who, whom) committed the robbery is in prison.

Whom   4. To (who, whom) am I speaking?

Who   5. (Who, Whom) did the lieutenant recommend for the position?

Who/who   6. (Who, Whom) hit (who, whom) first?

Who   7. The juvenile (who, whom) stole the car is in jail.

Whom   8. (Who, Whom) did the witness identify in the lineup?

Who   9. (Who, Whom) is going to roll call?

Who   10. (Who, Whom) was promoted?

Score = (correct × 10) = _____%

PART I

Proofreading

Rule to Remember

Writers of reports should always proofread their work before turning it in.

During the proofreading stage, you, the writer, should correct errors that pertain to the following:

- **grammar**
- **spelling**
- **punctuation**
- **capitalization**

Grammar Examples	Incorrect:	*Whom* do you think killed the victim?
	Correct:	*Who* do you think killed the victim?
Spelling Examples	Incorrect:	I found drug *paraphernelia* in the cell.
	Correct:	I found drug *paraphernalia* in the cell.
Punctuation Examples	Incorrect:	To relieve *stress Officer* Jones exercises in the evening.
	Correct:	To relieve *stress, Officer* Jones exercises in the evening.
Capitalization Examples	Incorrect:	The suspect was traveling *North* on the highway.
	Correct:	The suspect was traveling *north* on the highway.

Rules to Remember

Proofreading is a skill you can master if you adopt valid techniques and a vigorous approach to learning.

Consider these steps to help yourself and others improve:

R—**R**eview the report for content.
E—**E**valuate the report for errors.
A—**A**nalyze the report for clarity.
D—**D**etermine whether changes need to be made.

Exercise 1

Directions: Each sentence contains two mistakes. Underline the mistakes and correct them.

1. I heard allowed noise coming from the forth floor. *[a loud]* *[fourth]*
2. I patroled the area and spoted the fugitive. *[patrolled]* *[spotted]*
3. I transpoted the defendent to the station. *[transported]* *[defendant]*
4. The witness gives me a discription of the inmate. *[gave]* *[description]*
5. I found a suspected bag of marajuana in his right shirt pockit. *[marijuana]* *[pocket]*
6. I took know farther action. *[no]* *[further]*
7. The inmate had tools and counterfiet mony. *[counterfeit money]*
8. I saw no signs of forceable entree. *[forcible entry]*
9. He tells me he commited the arson. *[told]* *[committed]*
10. I saw the inmate drop a plastc bag to the ground; therefore, I retreived the bag. *[plastic]* *[retrieved]*

Score = (# correct × 10) = _____%

Exercise 2

Directions: Underline the words that are spelled incorrectly. Make the necessary corrections.

1. I patroled the area, and I obseved an armd robbry in progress.
2. I spoke to Leiutenant Brown about the disturbence.
3. Tommorow, I will be honured at the cerimony.
4. I seached the inmate's cell and siezed drug paraphernelia.
5. The inmate admited his involvment in the insident.
6. The offcer conficated six knifes from the vehicle.
7. Niether of the oficials is ready to speek to the media.
8. The victm is missing a gold neckless and a diamand earing.
9. Inmate Jones told investigaters he commited the assault.
10. Poofreading is a skill you can impove each and evry time you rite.

Score = (# correct × 10) = _____%

Exercise 3

Directions: Each sentence contains one error. Read each sentence *carefully*. On the blank provided, identify the error as follows: G (grammar), S (spelling), P (punctuation), or C (capitalization).

___S___ 1. I was patroling the downtown area.

___P___ 2. I asked the dispatcher to check the tag (XYZ 123) and she told me the car was stolen.

___P___ 3. When I asked the driver to step out of the car he hesitated momentarily.

___P___ 4. When he stepped out of the car, I searched him according to the standards of *Terry vs. Ohio*.

___S___ 5. Each of his pockets contained drug paraphernelia.

___S___ 6. I found a bag of marijana in his right pocket and a suspected cocaine rock in his left pocket.

___G___ 7. The suspect asked Officer Smith and I if she was under arrest.

___G___ 8. I arrested the suspect and reads him the Miranda warnings.

___G___ 9. I called the dispatcher whom said I could go to lunch.

___C___ 10. When I turned East, I spotted the fugitive's car.

Score = (# correct × 10) = _____%

Exercise 4

Directions: Each sentence contains one mistake. Read each sentence *carefully*. In the space provided, identify the error as follows: G (grammar), S (spelling), C (capitalization), or P (punctuation).

_____C_____ 1. The suspect was traveling South on I-95.

_____S_____ 2. Who is going to tommorow's seminar?

_____P_____ 3. The arson took place at 10.00 P.M.

_____P_____ 4. Arlington, Virginia is beautiful during December.

_____G_____ 5. Each of the officers ~~are~~ *is* scheduled for a vacation next week.

_____S_____ 6. The suspect's car has the following characteristics: It is brown, old, and dirty and has dents.

_____P_____ 7. Whom did the man ask for instruction's?

_____S_____ 8. In about ten minutes, the ~~imates~~ will eat lunch.

_____S_____ 9. The leiutenant asked him for his report.

_____C_____ 10. The annual report, submitted by major Davison, is on your desk.

Score = (# correct × 10) = _____%

Exercise 5

Directions: Carefully proofread the following poorly written narrative. Make the necessary grammar, spelling, punctuation, capitalization, word usage, and sentence structure corrections.

The Bad Police Report

I was ~~dispathed~~ *dispatched* to 8664 ~~oakwood~~ ~~avnue~~ *avenue* when E. Foster (~~victm~~ *victim*) ~~meets~~ *met* me in *the* front yard. Foster ~~tell~~ *told* me when he ~~arived~~ *arrived* home from work at 6:00 P.M., he ~~find~~ *found* the front door of the residents ~~unlock~~ *unlocked*. He then told me ~~that~~ when he *goes* ~~goes~~ inside the house, he ~~find~~ *found* his ~~sony~~ stereo system ~~missng~~ *missing*. He also told me when he ~~checked~~ *went* out his bedroom the dresser ~~draws~~ had been open. Also, $300 in cash and a mans 14 carrot gold neckless is missing.

E. Foster told me he lives ~~aloan~~ *alone*, ~~He~~ also ~~states~~ *stated* his nieghbor Al Louis often drops by unanounced. ~~I~~ checks out the doors and ~~win-dow~~ *windows* of the house and I observe ~~know~~ *no* sign of forceable entree.

AREA CANVAS

8668 oakwood avnue
8672 oakwood Avnue
8676 oakwood Avenew
8680 oakwood Avenue

Exercise 6

Directions: Carefully read the following poorly written narrative. Make the necessary grammar, spelling, punctuation, capitalization, word usage, and sentence structure corrections.

The Bad Corrections Report

On december 20,1994 at 1410 ours I conducts a pat seerch of imate Harry Foster ID#589921 in D Buiding. Imate Foster had returns from a vist with his wive Louise Foster in the visting loung of the facilty.

During my pat seerch of imate Fosters clotheing, I find these following items; a ten doller bill in Fosters left pants pockit and a Swiss army knive roled up in his write shirt sleve.

I ask imate Foster about the items I ask were he gets them. He says, its knot you're bussines, so shove it.

At approxmately 1415 hours I radio for assistence offcer Ben Griffin arrives at my location and escorded Imate Foster to confindment. I gives the ten dolar bill and the swiss army knive to Leiutenant Thomas Dalton. Leiutenant Dalton place the items to the contrabond safe. I takes no farther actions.

PART J

First-vs. Third-Person Reporting

Rules to Remember

An officer should document his or her actions by using the word *I*. This style of writing is called *first-person* reporting. Sometimes, an officer writes *this officer, this unit,* or *this reporter*. This style of writing is called *third-person reporting*. You should use the style your department recommends. Most training guidelines recommend *first-person reporting*.

Exercise 1

Directions: On the blank provided, place a (1) if the sentence is written in the first person. Place a (3) if the sentence is written in the third person.

_____3_____ 1. This unit arrived at the above location at 0900 hours.

_____1_____ 2. I arrived at the above location at 0900 hours.

_____1_____ 3. I questioned the juvenile about the incident.

_____3_____ 4. This reporter questioned the juvenile about the incident.

_____3_____ 5. This officer saw the inmate fleeing north.

_____1_____ 6. I saw the inmate fleeing north.

_____1_____ 7. I heard an inmate scream for help.

_____3_____ 8. This officer heard an inmate scream for help.

_____3_____ 9. This unit watched the cell for ten minutes.

_____1_____ 10. I watched the cell for ten minutes.

Score = (# correct × 10) = _____%

PART K

Report-Writing "Shoulds"

Rules to Remember

1. Reports <u>should</u> include the following essential components:

   WHO

   a. Who is the victim?
   b. Who are the witnesses?
   c. Who is the suspect?

   WHAT

   a. What type of offense has been committed?
   b. What is the classification of the offense (felony, misdemeanor)?
   c. What happened?

   WHEN

   a. When did you arrive?
   b. When did the offense take place (date, time)?
   c. When was the crime first discovered?

   WHERE

   a. Where was the offense committed?
   b. Where is the specific address of the area?
   c. Where is the suspect?

WHY

a. Why did the suspect commit the offense?
b. Why was the victim involved?
c. Why was the offense reported?

How

a. How was the offense committed?
b. How many items were stolen?
c. How many victims, witnesses, and suspects were involved?

2. Reports should consist of words that are <u>clear</u> and <u>*familiar*</u>. Your job is to <u>express</u> information. Your job is not to <u>impress</u> the reader. Consider the following words:

Fire   or   Conflagration
Crowd   or   Confluence
Agree   or   Concurrence

Now consider the following sentence:

a. The <u>crowd agreed</u> to move away from the fire.
b. The <u>confluence</u> was in <u>concurrence</u> about moving away from the <u>conflagration</u>.

Which sentence is <u>appropriate</u> for a report?
Sentence.

3. Reports *should* be written in the *first person*.

Examples: *I* spoke with the victim who told me. . . .
I responded to a robbery call.
I arrested the suspect.

4. Reports *should* be *grammatically* correct.

singular subjects = singular verbs
plural subjects = plural verbs

5. Reports *should* be written in the *active voice*.

Examples:

(Active) *I wrote* the ticket.
(Passive) The ticket *was written* by *me*.

PART L

Note Taking

Rules to Remember

Good notes are essential for factual, accurate reports. The *A-B-C-D-E-F* system will be very helpful to you when you start the communication process of taking notes. Note that many report writers use bullets (•) to highlight important themes. Bullets are effective because they save the writer time. Ask a representative from your department if bullet style is acceptable on your reports. Organize your notes in the following manner.

Step A—Actions
(officer's)

Start your narrative with a standard introductory line:
On the above date and time, I, Officer John Miller, was dispatched to 4763 Arborwood Road regarding an armed robbery.
■ What type of offense are you investigating?
■ Were you dispatched to the scene?
■ Were you on your shift when you saw or heard something?

Step B—Behavior
(witness's, suspect's, victim's)

■ Be observant!
■ Be specific!
■ Do not draw conclusions!
■ If you see bruise marks, are you going to write, "Suspect inflicted bruises"? Not if you did not <u>see</u> the suspect inflict the bruises. Instead you would write:

Examples: ■ I noticed bruise marks on Smith's upper right arm. Smith told me her boyfriend punched her on the arm.

■ This statement describes, in a specific manner, what you saw. It is not based upon a conclusion.

■ If the suspect acts hostile, are you going to write, "Suspect acted in a hostile manner"? No! Instead, in your narrative, you will explain the behavior.

Step C—Communication
(dialogue, questions, answers)   Ask questions and follow-up questions.

Example: *Officer Miller:*   "Mr. Brown, please tell me what you saw."

Mr. Brown: "I saw a white male in his early thirties holding a black trench coat and black hat. When he left the bank, I saw him carrying a white sack under the coat. He had something green on his face. It looked like green paint on his face."

Follow-up question

Officer Miller: "Mr. Brown, did you say you 'saw' a white sack?"

Mr. Brown: "Yes, I saw it—under his coat."

Follow-up question

Officer Miller: "You said the color on his face was. . . ."

Mr. Brown: "Green. He had green paint on his face."

Step D—Description
(scene, suspect)

■ Once again, your observations are important!
■ Keep your eyes open!
■ Listen for unusual sounds!

Examples:

- While I was patrolling the downtown area, I saw the suspect weave in and out of three lanes of traffic.
- When I arrived at 7105 Pine Wood Avenue, I saw three males wrestling on the ground. They were punching and kicking each other.
- While patrolling the Shady Meadows area, I heard a woman scream, "9-1-1 call the police! He took my purse!"
- Jones (witness) told me the suspect was wearing a red tank top with the number 13, yellow shorts, and white tennis shoes. Jones described the suspect as a fifteen-year-old Anglo male with brown hair and brown eyes. He is approximately five feet, eight inches tall and has a tattoo on his left arm that reads "Jenny."

Step E—Evidence
(tangibles, prints, statements)

- Look for key pieces of evidence.
- Be observant.
- Record and document key facts.

Example:

When I arrived at 35790 Dixie Way, I saw broken glass on the porch of the house. A large rock was close by. As I continued to search the area, I found the side door (south entrance to the house) spray painted in red letters: PWR.

Step F—Final Disposition
(resolution)

- How did you resolve the matter?
- What was your final action?

Examples:

- I arrested the suspect.
- I read the suspect the Miranda warnings from my card.
- I transported the suspect to the station.
- I gave Wilson a domestic violence pamphlet.
- I explained state attorney procedures to Wilson.
- I took no further action.

Remember that the *A-B-C-D-E-F* system will help you in the note-taking phase of communicating.

Now see how it helps you in writing your field notes.

Sample Notes: Domestic Violence Case

A—Actions

- I was dispatched to 8872 Timber Lane regarding a domestic violence call.
- Date: April 18, 1996
- Dispatch time: 1604 hours
- Arrival time: 1610 hours

B—Behavior

Lucy Monroe (victim) screamed, "Officer, help me. He's going to kill me!"
Lucy Monroe:
- Shaky hands
- Trembling body
- Messy hair
- Red marks (large marks on face and neck)

C—Communication

- Scott Russo (neighbor) heard noises.
- "Loud crashing noises"
- Coming from Monroe house

D—Description

- Jack Monroe (suspect)
- Smoking a cigarette
- Sweating
- Ice pack on hand

E—Evidence

- Broken lamp shade (living room floor)
- Broken glasses (kitchen floor)
- Broken dishes (kitchen floor)
- Q: "What happened to your wife's face?"
- A: J. Monroe—"I punched her."

F—Final Disposition

- I arrested J. Monroe.
- I read Miranda warnings to J. Monroe.
- I gave L. Monroe a domestic violence pamphlet and case card.
- I explained state attorney procedures to L. Monroe.
- I took no further police action.

PART M

Organizing the Report

Rule to Remember

When writing the report, organize your narrative according to the
A-B-C-D-E-F system.

> (officer's) ***Actions***
> (witness's, suspect's, victim's) ***Behavior***
> (dialogue, questions, answers) ***Communication***
> (scene, suspect) ***Description***
> (tangibles, prints, statements) ***Evidence***
> (resolution) ***Final Disposition***

Here is sample domestic-violence narrative, which is organized
according to the *A-B-C-D-E-F* system.

Actions: On the above date and time, I, Officer Mark Thompson, was
dispatched to 8872 Timber Lane regarding a domestic violence call.

Behavior: When I arrived, Lucy Monroe (victim) screamed, "Officer,
help me! He's going to kill me!" I noticed L. Monroe's body was
shaking. Her hands were trembling, her hair was messy, and I saw
large red marks on her neck and face.

Communication: L. Monroe's neighbor, Scott Russo, told me he
heard screams coming from the Monroe house and "loud crashing
noises."

Description: L. Monroe and I entered the house, where I saw Jack
Monroe (suspect) smoking a cigarette. He was sweating and had an
ice pack on his hand.

Evidence: When I asked J. Monroe what happened to his wife's
face, he said, "I punched her." As I looked around the Monroe home,
I saw a broken lamp shade on the living room floor and broken
glasses and dishes on the kitchen floor.

Final Disposition: I arrested J. Monroe and read him the Miranda
rights from my card. I gave L. Monroe a domestic violence pamphlet
and a case card. I explained state attorney procedures to L. Monroe.

PART N

Observation and Description

Rule to Remember

Your ability to observe what you saw and then describe it in the report is a critical skill. On a daily basis, you will need to describe persons, places, things, behaviors, and appearances.

Describing Suspects

Observation skills and memory are crucial for any report writer. What is certainly challenging is trying to get other parties (witnesses and victims) to heighten their observation and memory skills, especially when you are the reporting officer and you must rely upon what others are telling you.

Here are some helpful ways to extract critical, descriptive information from witnesses and victims and help them remember information that will be vital to the investigation.

1. *Ask the person to describe the individual.* What does the person look like? This open-ended question allows each witness or victim to first recall everything he or she easily can about the potential suspect.

2. *Ask very specific questions about the suspect individual (from top to bottom).* Lead with these detail-directed questions:

   a. Do you remember what color hair the suspect has?
   b. Is it wavy or straight?
   c. Is it short cropped, medium length, or long?

3. *Ask the person to describe any prominent facial features.* Ask for features such as these:

   a. Acne?
   b. Birth marks?
   c. Facial hair?
   d. Eye color?
   e. Eye shape?
   f. Teeth (missing, braces, gold fillings)?

4. *Ask the person for a description of body type.* Lead with these details:

   a. Slim?
   b. Medium build?
   c. Heavy?
   d. Obese?

5. *Ask for a description of height.* A good rule of thumb is to have the victim or witness look at your height and then ask her or him if the suspect is about the same height, taller, or shorter than you are.

6. *Ask for a description of clothing.* Lead by asking about these specifics:

   a. Color of shirt/dress/jacket?
   b. Color of pants/slacks?
   c. Color of shoes?
   d. Color of hat (if applicable)?

7. *Ask for a description of the vehicle the person may have been driving.* Details include these:

   a. Make?
   b. Model?
   c. Color?
   d. Approximate year?
   e. Any letters/numbers of license plate?

The following exercise will help you improve your descriptive ability and record what you observe in a clear and specific manner.

Exercise 1

Directions: Give descriptive details for the following.

1. Juvenile _____

_____

2. Car _____

_____

3. Watch _____

_____

4. Suspect's clothing _____

_____

5. Defendant's physical appearance _____

_____

6. Tattoo _____

_____

7. Height and weight of victim _____

_____

8. Inmate's attitude and demeanor _____

_____

9. Time of day _____

_____

10. Defendant's hostile behavior _____

_____

Score = (# correct × 10) = _____%

PART 0

Your A–Z Guide at a Glance

A—*A*lways record the facts.

B—*B*e mindful of grammar, punctuation, and sentence structure.

C—*C*heck your work before turning it in.

D—*D*escribe the situation.

E—*E*dit your report.

F—*F*irst-person reporting is crucial. (Use "I" instead of "This officer.")

G—*G*ather your notes in a notebook.

H—*H*ave an organized plan when writing.

I—*I*nclude who, what, when, where, why, and how.

J—*J*ust the facts are needed! (no opinions).

K—*K*eep it simple.

L—*L*eave no stone unturned. (Include everything that's pertinent to the case.)

M—*M*ake sure the report is accurate and factual.

N—*N*o mistakes are allowed!

O—*O*pinions aren't included.

P—*P*roofread your report.

Q—*Q*uit bad writing habits.

R—*R*eview your report before turning it in.

S—*S*pell all words correctly.

T—*T*ake writing your report seriously.

U—*U*nderestimating the importance of good report writing will have negative implications.

V—*V*ery important: Use the right forms (i.e., arrest, incident).

W—*W*riting a good report will aid you in court.

X—*Ex*tra practice will help you improve your skills.

Y—*Y*ou can write good reports if you try!

Z—*Z*ap all errors before you submit your report.

PART P

Report-Writing Exercises for Police, Probation, and Corrections Officers

Sample Police Reports

Case 1

DOMESTIC DISPUTE

Directions: Read the following information. Assume that you have been dispatched to the call. In the space provided, write five questions you would ask the victim and five questions you would ask the suspect. Then write a report narrative.

You arrive at Cheap & Cozy Apartments when a white female, EMILY SHERMAN (VICTIM), meets you outside by the front door. E. SHERMAN'S hair is messy, and her left shirt sleeve is torn. You immediately notice that her right eye is swollen. You question E. SHERMAN, who tells you that her husband, GARY SHERMAN (SUSPECT), punched her in the face when she confronted him about his alleged gambling and drinking problem. E. SHERMAN tells you that her husband has a violent temper and that he frequently "beats her" when he has been drinking.

E. SHERMAN allows you to enter her apartment. Once inside, you observe G. SHERMAN pacing the kitchen floor. He is drinking a can of beer. When he sees you, he yells, "Get the hell outta here, cop!" You question G. SHERMAN, who says his wife is a "crazy woman" and that she should be taken to the "funny farm." G. SHERMAN has nothing else to say to you.

As you conclude the narrative, include the steps you would take in resolving this dispute.

Write five questions you would ask Emily Sherman (victim).

1. _____

_____

2. _____

_____

3. _____

_____

4. _____

_____

5. _____

_____

Write five questions you would ask Gary Sherman (suspect).

1. _____

_____

2. _____

_____

3. _____

_____

4. _____

_____

5. _____

_____

Domestic Dispute Narrative

Case 2

Burglary

Directions: Read the following information. Assume you have been dispatched to the call. In the space provided, write ten questions you would ask the victim. Then write a report narrative.

You arrive at 56788 Lakefront Drive when a black male, who identifies himself as EDDIE HANSON (VICTIM), meets you in the front yard. HANSON tells you that when he arrived home from work at 6:00 P.M., he found the front door to his house unlocked. He then tells you that when he went inside the house, he found his Sony stereo system "gone." He adds that when he checked his bedroom, he found the bureau drawers open and $500 in cash missing. HANSON also tells you that a man's 14 carat gold ring was missing.

HANSON says he lives alone, but he tells you his cousin, LEONARD JONES, sometimes drops by unannounced. HANSON tells you that JONES has his own key. You check the doors and windows to the house. You observe no signs of forced entry.

You conduct an area canvass, which produces negative results.

AREA CANVASS:

56790 Lakefront Drive
56792 Lakefront Drive
56794 Lakefront Drive
56796 Lakefront Drive

Write ten questions you would ask Eddie Hanson (victim).

1. _____

   _____

2. _____

   _____

3. _____

   _____

4. _____

   _____

5. _____

   _____

6. _____

   _____

7. _____

   _____

8. _____

   _____

9. _____

   _____

10. _____

   _____

Burglary Narrative

_____
_____
_____
_____
_____
_____
_____
_____
_____
_____
_____
_____
_____
_____
_____
_____
_____
_____
_____
_____
_____
_____
_____
_____
_____
_____
_____
_____
_____
_____
_____
_____
_____
_____
_____
_____

Case 3

AGGRAVATED BATTERY

Directions: Read the following information. Assume you have been dispatched to the call. Write five questions you would ask the victim, the witness, and the suspect. Then write a report narrative.

You arrive at the Lovely Lady Lounge and see a white male, BOB DELANEY (VICTIM), lying on the pavement. A white female, RENEE ROGERS (WITNESS), tells you that her boyfriend (DELANEY) and a patron JAY MONTGOMERY (SUSPECT) started arguing while they were watching the show at Lovely Lady Lounge. ROGERS tells you that DELANEY and MONTGOMERY stepped outside to the parking lot where MONTGOMERY punched DELANEY in the abdomen and hit him in the nose. ROGERS adds that DELANEY fell to the ground when MONTGOMERY struck him in the head, approximately four times, with a piece of wood.

You enter the bar to question the patrons, but you soon find out that nobody saw or heard anything. MONTGOMERY steps forth to tell you that DELANEY has a "big, fat mouth" and that somebody needed to tell him to "shut it." You ask MONTGOMERY if he struck DELANEY. MONTGOMERY replies, "Yeah, and what are *you* going to do about it?"

Aggravated Battery

Write five questions you would ask Bob Delaney (victim).

1. _____

2. _____

3. _____

4. _____

5. _____

Write five questions you would ask Renee Rogers (witness).

1. _____
2. _____
3. _____
4. _____
5. _____

Write five questions you would ask Jay Montgomery (suspect).

1. _____
2. _____
3. _____
4. _____
5. _____

Aggravated Battery Narrative

_____

_____

_____

_____

_____

_____

_____

_____

_____

_____

_____

_____

_____

_____

_____

_____

_____

_____

_____

_____

_____

_____

_____

_____

_____

_____

_____

_____

_____

_____

_____

_____

_____

SAMPLE CORRECTIONS REPORTS

Case 1

FRISK SEARCH

Directions: Read the following information. In the space provided, write five questions you would ask Inmate Larry Bradford, and write five things you would tell the shift commander. Then write a report narrative using only the information provided in the scenario, and write five things you would tell the shift commander.

On December 23, 1993, at 1414 hours, Inmate Larry Bradford, ID# 589921, returns to D building after visiting his wife, Henrietta Bradford, in the Family Lounge of the facility. At 1415 hours, you conduct a frisk search of Inmate Bradford's clothing in D Building.

During your search of Inmate Bradford, you find a $20 bill in Bradford's right pants pocket and a Swiss Army knife in his left pants pocket.

You ask Bradford about the items and where he had gotten them. He replies, "It ain't none of your damn business, so shove it."

At 1417 hours, you radio for assistance. Officer Samuel Griffin arrives at your post and escorts Inmate Larry Bradford to confinement. You give the $20 bill and the Swiss Army knife to Lieutenant Thomas Johnson, who places the items into the contraband safe. You take no further action.

Write five questions you would ask Inmate Larry Bradford.

1. _____

_____

2. _____

_____

3. _____

_____

4. _____

_____

5. _____

_____

Write five things you would tell the shift commander about this incident.

1. _____

_____

2. _____

_____

3. _____

_____

4. _____

_____

5. _____

_____

Frisk Search Narrative

Case 2

ATTEMPTED ASSAULT OR BATTERY WITH A DEADLY WEAPON

Directions: Read the following information. In the space provided, write five questions you would ask Inmate Ronald Hopkins, write five questions you would ask Inmate Mark Davis, and write five things you would tell the officer in charge. Then write a report narrative using the information in the scenario.

On April 8, 1994, at approximately 1900 hours, you witness Inmate Ronald Hopkins, ID# 377649, running after Inmate Mark Davis, ID# 462215, in the kitchen. Inmates Hopkins and Davis are assigned to kitchen duty. You see a shiny metal object in Inmate Hopkins's hand. You believe the object is a knife. You call for backup. At approximately 1902 hours, Sergeant Tim Jackson, Officer George Taylor, and Officer John Jones arrive at your location. Everyone observes Inmate Hopkins attempt to stab Inmate Davis in the stomach. You order Inmate Hopkins to drop the knife, which is approximately four inches long. He does. You secure the knife. At approximately 1903 hours, Officers Taylor and Jones apply restraints to Inmate Hopkins's wrists. Sergeant Jackson questions Inmate Davis. Inmate Davis has no visible signs of injury and states that he is not injured. Officer Jones escorts Inmate Hopkins to confinement.

At 1905 hours, Lieutenant Ben Wilson contacts the police department. Inmate Davis presses charges. Officer Max Reynolds (#6784) arrives at 1925 hours. You give Officer Reynolds the evidence. You take no further action.

Write five questions you would ask Inmate Ronald Hopkins.

1. _____

_____

2. _____

_____

3. _____

_____

4. _____

_____

5. _____

_____

Write five questions you would ask Inmate Mark Davis.

1. _____
   _____

2. _____
   _____

3. _____
   _____

4. _____
   _____

5. _____
   _____

Write five things you would tell the officer in charge.

1. _____
   _____

2. _____
   _____

3. _____
   _____

4. _____
   _____

5. _____
   _____

Attempted Assault or Battery Narrative

_____
_____
_____
_____
_____
_____
_____
_____
_____
_____
_____
_____
_____
_____
_____
_____
_____
_____
_____
_____
_____
_____
_____
_____
_____
_____
_____
_____
_____
_____
_____
_____
_____
_____
_____
_____
_____
_____

Case 3

Disobeying Verbal or Written Orders

Directions: Read the following information. In the space provided, write five questions that you would ask Inmate William Durand. Then write a report narrative using the information in the scenario.

On August 21, 1993, at 1105 hours, you are assigned as the dormitory officer for E Building. At approximately 1107 hours, you order Inmate William Durand, ID# 763345, to leave E Building and report to his assigned work post. On this day, Inmate Durand is assigned to yard duty, and he has not been given permission to be in the building. However, he is in the building watching a football game on TV. You tell Inmate Durand, "Report to yard duty now." Inmate Durand says, "No way, man. I want to see who wins." You respond, "I order you to leave this building and report to yard duty now." Inmate Durand replies, "You report to yard duty."

You notify the officer in charge about the incident. At approximately 1109 hours, you remove Inmate Durand from trusty status. Officer Karl Mosley arrives and escorts Inmate Durand to a nontrusty dormitory. You take no further action.

Write five questions you would ask Inmate William Durand.

1. _____

_____

2. _____

_____

3. _____

_____

4. _____

_____

5. _____

_____

Disobeying Verbal or Written Orders Narrative

_____

_____

_____

_____

_____

_____

_____

_____

_____

_____

_____

_____

_____

_____

_____

_____

_____

_____

_____

_____

_____

_____

_____

_____

_____

_____

_____

_____

_____

_____

_____

_____

_____

_____

Sample Presentence Investigation Report

Directions: Review the following information. In the space provided on a subsequent page, write questions that you would ask the defendant about the incident. Write an evaluation summary as in Part V based upon the information provided.

I. Data

Name:	Ford, Michael Jeffrey	**Date:**	August 18, 1994
Address:	11890 Freemont Lane Miami, FL	**Docket No.:**	94-529
		Offense:	Grand theft
Home Phone:	(305) 990-2041	**Penalty:**	3 to 5 years
Legal Residence:	Same	**Plea:**	Guilty
Age:	26	**Custody:**	Released on own recognizance
Date of Birth:	May 9, 1968		
Place of Birth:	Miami, FL	**Prosecutor:**	Bernard Johnson
Sex:	Male		
Race:	Caucasian	**Defense Atty:**	Susan Mitchell
Citizenship:	U.S.		
Education:	12th Grade	**Drug/Alcohol Involvement:**	None
Social Security No:	536-86-0056		
Prior Record:	None		

II. Official Version of the Offense

On July 9, 1994, at 3:30 P.M., the defendant entered The Athletic Company sporting goods store located in Plaza Mall. The store manager saw the defendant walk around the store and look at various types of sneakers. The manager approached the defendant and asked if he could be of assistance. The defendant said, "I'd like to try on Nike sneakers. I need about five pairs in size 10." The manager brought the defendant three pairs of running shoes and two pairs of tennis shoes. The defendant requested a sixth pair of sneakers. At that time, the manager went to the supply area, located in the back of the store. While the manager was in the supply area, the defendant exited The Athletic Company. He took the five pairs of shoes and did not pay for the merchandise. The manager called for assistance. The on-duty police officer caught up with the defendant in the parking lot. The officer arrested the defendant and transported him to the jail. The stolen merchandise was valued at $374.95.

III. Defendant's Version of the Offense

During my meeting with the defendant, I questioned him regarding the events of July 9, 1994. The defendant readily admitted his participation in the crime. He explained that he felt pressured to steal the merchandise. He intended to sell the items to "friends" in order to pay for his rent. In addition, the defendant has a seven-year-old son whom his ex-wife is raising. The defendant said he also took the merchandise so he could have enough money to take his son camping. The defendant is truly remorseful about his actions. He is embarrassed for himself and his family. He would like the opportunity to make up for his behavior.

IV. Personal History

The defendant was born in Miami, Florida, on May 9, 1968, and he is an only child. The defendant attended the Dade County Public School System from grades K-12. He was involved in cross-country running and band during his high school years. He graduated high school with a 2.6 grade point average.

The defendant's parents have been married for twenty-nine years. His father, Donald, is employed as a mechanic for the airlines. He has a high school diploma and two years of community college education. His mother, Rebecca, is employed as a part-time teaching assistant. She is currently attending classes at the local college, where she is studying elementary education.

When the defendant completed high school, he enrolled in the local community college, where he met his ex-wife, Diane Anderson. They had dated for six months when she became pregnant. The defendant dropped out of school and married Diane. To support his family, he worked full-time as a cashier in a liquor store. They married on June 3, 1987. The marriage lasted three years. He maintains a friendship with his ex-wife, who has custody of their son, Michael, Jr.

The defendant is in excellent physical health. He exercises three times a week at the gymnasium. He has no illnesses, yet he states he becomes depressed when he thinks about "his life." The defendant would like to receive counseling, and his ex-wife stated that she would attend sessions with him.

The defendant is presently employed at a bowling alley. His manager and fellow employees commented that he is "responsible" and "easy to get along with."

V. Evaluation Summary

The defendant is a twenty-six-year-old Caucasian male who entered a plea of guilty to grand theft. He admitted stealing five pairs of Nike sneakers, which he had hoped to sell for cash. He wanted to pay his rent and take his child camping.

The defendant's parents and ex-wife are supportive, and they are willing to help him "get back on his feet." He has a high school diploma and is presently employed. He is deeply remorseful and embarrassed about his actions.

VI. Recommendation

I respectfully recommend that the court grant the defendant admission to probation. The defendant has no prior record, he has a supportive family, and he would like to participate in counseling, both alone and with his ex-wife. He is committed to improving the quality of his life, and he eagerly anticipates an opportunity to make up for his actions.

Respectfully,
Gerald R. Hughes
Probation Officer

Directions: In the space provided, write questions that you would ask the defendant about the incident. Write an evaluation summary as in Part V on the next page.

1. _____

_____

2. _____

_____

3. _____

_____

4. _____

_____

5. _____

_____

Evaluation Summary Narrative

_____

_____

_____

_____

_____

_____

_____

_____

_____

_____

_____

_____

_____

_____

_____

_____

_____

_____

_____

_____

_____

_____

_____

_____

_____

_____

_____

_____

_____

_____

_____

PART Q

Interviewing Skills and Investigative Reporting

The *investigation* is a critical component in the report-writing process. It is composed of the following:

1. *An investigator.*

This individual is responsible for analyzing situations and facts to determine what happened and what crime, if any, occurred. The investigator asks questions, conducts interviews, collects evidence, develops informants, examines crime scenes, and explores any and all relevant evidence to help him or her determine what has occurred in a given situation.

2. *The investigation.*

The investigation itself is the process of conducting a lawful search of people, property, or things to determine who did what to whom, when, where, how, and why.

It is fair to say that the investigation is conducted when law enforcement has *reason to believe* that a crime has occurred or believes a crime is going to occur.

An investigator should consider a variety of good questions in almost every circumstance:

1. Who are my reporting party, victim, witness, and suspect?
2. What happened?
3. Where did the incident occur?
4. When did the incident occur?
5. Why did this crime take place? (motivation of offender)
6. How did the incident occur?

All investigators throughout the United States and abroad should have the following traits to succeed in the job:

1. Credible
2. Ethical
3. Highly motivated and committed
4. Acutely aware of facts, circumstances, surroundings, and parties involved
5. Intellectually inclined to piece together the puzzles to solve a crime
6. Analytical
7. Tireless
8. Professional
9. Able to communicate effectively
10. Dedicated

A successful investigation can lead to the solid conviction of a defendant. A weak investigation can lead to the unraveling of a case. The investigation is a critical step in the report-writing process for the beginning or veteran officer.

PART R

Ten Steps for Becoming a Good Listener

Every criminal justice professional has what it takes to be a good listener. The issue is whether you want to be a good listener? Are you willing to take a few easy steps to become an effective listener?

If so, consider these ten steps for becoming an effective listener:

1. Look at the person who is speaking.
2. Do not interrupt!
3. Be mindful of your nonverbal signals when you communicate.
4. Concentrate on what the person is saying.
5. Display courtesy, professionalism, and respect (CPR).
6. Appear interested, cooperative, and open.
7. Ask questions.
8. View the other person as having something worthwhile to say.
9. Take notes.
10. Practice, practice, practice!

Listening is an extremely important process in the entire communication exchange. It really is a skill that can be easily acquired if you are willing to work at it each day for the rest of your career.

PART 5

CPR–Courtesy, Professionalism, and Respect

Officer, I'd like to be the first one to let you know that I truly respect, appreciate, and admire the fine work you do. I also fully understand the complex, challenging nature of your job and the enormous stress you face on a daily basis.

In spite of this, I'd like to remind you that it is extremely important each and every single time you communicate with each person with whom you have contact to always practice *CPR: Courtesy, Professionalism, and Respect*. Doing so will have several distinct advantages for you.

1. Lead to effective interactions with others.
2. Put other people at ease.
3. Help others communicate in a similar manner.
4. Promote self-discipline.
5. Remind you that you are in control no matter who is losing control around you.

PART T

Establishing Rapport

Rapport refers to a relationship marked by harmony or affinity. It enables you to establish a level of comfort and trust with a party you may need information from: victim, witness, reporting party, or suspect. Establishing rapport is a critical skill for every officer, investigator, and report writer.

Here are some easy-to-use tips for establishing rapport.

1. *Always introduce yourself.* Don't assume because you are wearing a uniform (or professional business attire for a detective or investigator) that this identifies you. Say: "Good Morning (Sir/Madam). My name is Officer/Detective (your name) from the (name of your department)."
2. *Tell the individual with whom you are speaking that you are here to help him or her.* This is very important! Many people feel nervous and uncomfortable in the presence of a police officer. For a variety of reasons, many (even if they've done nothing wrong) experience a level of intimidation.
3. *If possible, offer the person with whom you are speaking food, a beverage, or even a cigarette.* This is a technique that is especially helpful to investigators before interrogating a potential suspect! A very good friend of mine, who has been a homicide detective for more than thirty years in Miami, Florida, says this "works like a charm." He'll say to a suspect, "Hey, listen, I'm kind of hungry, and I'm going to order lunch. What can I get you?" My detective friend says all of a sudden the guy or gal who thinks he's the enemy is taken aback and starts to relax a bit by this small act of kindness. The suspect will say, "I'll have a sub sandwich, chips, and a coke." My friend says, "This $5 dollar investment is worth its weight in gold toward establishing rapport with someone from whom I need information."

4. *Tell the person you need his or her help.* Sometimes people are extremely reluctant to speak with you. Of course, it's nothing personal; you're a cop and they may be uncomfortable around you. Tell each person, "Look, this is a really serious crime we've got here. I can't do this without you. I need your help." It's a very sincere, direct way to establish rapport with a victim, witness, or suspect.

PART U

Interpersonal Communication

As an officer, your ability to communicate effectively with every individual with whom you come into contact is crucial to your role in criminal justice, as well as your professional report-writing responsibility. Therefore, you should always remember that both written and oral communications are essential to your success in the profession.

Oral communication occurs daily when you communicate with:

1. Citizens
2. Victims, witnesses, and suspects
3. Fellow officers
4. Attorneys
5. Supervisors

Written communication is displayed every time you fill out various reports and write report narratives, department policies, and memorandums.

The essential rule of thumb to remember is that all communication, whether written or oral, must be:

1. *Clear*
2. *Concise*
3. *Complete*
4. *Correct*

If one element of the four is lacking, the quality will undoubtedly suffer.

PART V

Nonverbal Communication

We've all heard the expression, "It's not *what* you say but *how* you say it." This is true; however, I maintain that in large part we communicate volumes by what we *don't* say and how we nonverbally communicate. As you are aware, nonverbal communication takes many forms:

1. *Posture (straight or slumped?)*
2. *Facial expressions (relaxed or stressed?)*
3. *Arms (folded or relaxed?)*
4. *Eye contact (direct or darting around?)*
5. *Legs (crossed or uncrossed?)*

The more familiar you become with your own nonverbal gestures as well as those of others, the more insight you will have into how open or closed another party is.

PART W

When to Write a Report

You will encounter many types of incidents, offenses, and crimes during your profession. Each one will require a report. This is not a comprehensive list by any means, but it represents a type of checklist for you.

Write a report if you are the reporting officer involved in a:

1. Murder
2. Rape
3. Robbery
4. Aggravated assault
5. Larceny/theft
6. Burglary
7. Motor vehicle theft
8. Arson

Obviously, these are the Part I crimes in the U.C.R.

You will encounter a number of other incidents, as well as Part II crimes. You will be writing arrest reports, incident reports, supplemental reports, and log sheets.

As you progress through the ranks and seek promotion, you may be called upon to write memorandums and policies for your department. The bottom line is this: **Writing a report is a critically crucial aspect of the profession, so do it well each and every time!**

PART X

The Four C's

The four C's of report writing are the same as those for all communication:

1. *Clear*
2. *Concise*
3. *Complete*
4. *Correct*

When a report contains direct, straightforward, easy-to-understand language (not jargon), it is considered **clear**.

Unclear Example:	I verbally articulated to the defendant that his ability to move about freely had been curtailed immediately.
	(Excuse me? What did you do?)
Clear Example:	I told the defendant he was under arrest.
	(Much better, right?)

When a report is brief yet factual, it is considered **concise**. Remember that brevity is often (but not always) best. It depends on the situation. For example, the nature of the circumstances and the volume of information that must be reported cause many traffic and homicide narrative reports to be lengthy. A long report must still be concise.

Concise Example:	I transported the suspect to the station.
Wordy Example:	I proceeded to transport via patrol vehicle said suspect to the station.

A report is considered *complete* when all answers to basic questions have been addressed: who, what, when, where, why, and how.

Complete Example: On January 1, 2006, (**when**) I interviewed Victim Sally Smith (**who**) at 1234 Park Lane (**where**). The victim informed me that her husband, Suspect Jack Smith (**who**), punched (**how**) her in the right eye because she was late coming home from work (**why**).

Incomplete Example: Victim Smith was interviewed regarding being punched in the right eye.

A report is *correct* when it has no errors pertaining to the facts, spelling, grammar, sentence structure, and punctuation.

Correct Example: I received a call from the dispatcher regarding a reported domestic violence incident.

Incorrect Example: I recieved a call from the dispatcher regarding a reported domestic violence incident.

PART Y

Document, Document, Document

Officer, I will be brief and simply remind you that it is critical to document as much detail as you can (usually in a notebook or field book) so that your report will be the four things we just reviewed in Part X: clear, concise, complete, and correct. You may face a great deal of day-to-day pressure. By documenting the facts and circumstances of an incident or crime in an organized manner, you will find this approach to be extremely helpful to you.

PART Z

Get a Writing Mentor

A writing mentor does not have to be someone who has a bachelor's, master's, or doctoral degree in English. A writing mentor is someone in your profession, perhaps a fellow officer or supervisor, whose writing style is factual, clear, and professional. This should be an individual who knows about all facets of report writing, performs this aspect of the job well, has a positive attitude, and is willing to help others.

If you think about it, most of us have had mentors along the way who have provided guidance, advice, and direction most likely during critical stages in our personal lives as well as in our careers.

I believe that having a writing mentor could be a really significant step for someone who is truly serious about writing quality reports. After all, you may write each day for the rest of your career. Have someone help you now, and this could save you a great deal of time and unnecessary headaches in the future.

Author's Note

Ladies and gentlemen, I hope you found Section 1, The A–Z's of Report Writing, helpful because my goal is to remind you of all of the critical steps involved in the report-writing process. Obviously, we agree that this is a crucial aspect of your performance as a criminal justice professional. In the upcoming sections, I would like to review with you the elements of *good writing.*

It is my assumption that you are already a quality writer; however, even the best writers need a refresher from time to time (including me!).

SECTION II

Parts of Speech

In many of life's experiences, we are asked to perform a role that could have an important impact upon the functioning of a larger unit. For example, a police officer must make a lawful arrest before a defendant can move into the judicial environment. When a judge renders a verdict and sentences a defendant to serve time in a confined facility, correctional officers must perform their roles by ensuring custody, care, and control. Therefore, in order for the criminal justice system to operate efficiently, all participants must perform their duties in an efficient manner. The same thinking can be applied to the function of the words in a sentence: Various words in a sentence must work together and perform a necessary role in order to ensure a clear well-communicated message.

In this section, we will explore the roles of the eight **parts of speech**, which identify the type of function each word has in a sentence:

1. Nouns
2. Pronouns
3. Verbs
4. Adjectives
5. Adverbs
6. Prepositions
7. Conjunctions
8. Interjections

PART A

Nouns

Rule to Remember

The noun's role or function in a sentence is to name something. A noun names a person, place, thing, action, quality, or belief.

Nouns can be broken into five categories:

1. **Concrete**
2. **Proper**
3. **Common**
4. **Collective**
5. **Abstract**

1. Concrete Nouns

Rule to Remember

A concrete noun identifies something tangible that is perceived through the senses. If you can see it, hear it, smell it, taste it, or touch it, the word is most likely a concrete noun.

Examples:

The *badge* is silver. The *uniform* is impressive.
The *bullet* is cold. The *radio* is new.

Badge, bullet, uniform, and *radio* are **concrete nouns.**

2. Proper Nouns

Rule to Remember

A proper noun names specific people, things, or places.

Examples:

Chief Thomas Jackson is the keynote speaker.
Special Agent Hernandez is retiring next month.
Judge Goldberg is highly respected in this community.
Miami, Florida, is a great place to live.
Miami-Dade Police Department employs professional personnel.

Chief Thomas Jackson, Special Agent Hernandez, Judge Goldberg, Miami, Florida, and *Miami-Dade Police Department* are proper nouns.

Note: Proper nouns are capitalized because they are the names of specific people, places, or things.

3. Common Nouns

Rule to Remember

A common noun is a word that does not identify specific people, things, or places.

Examples:

The *judge* is impartial.   The *major* is a fair administrator.
The *juror* asked a question.   The *inmate* spoke to his attorney.

Judge, juror, major, and *inmate* are common nouns.

Note: Common nouns are *not* capitalized because they do *not* name specific people, things, or places.

4. Collective Nouns

Rule to Remember

A collective noun names a group of people or a group of things that belong to a whole.

Examples:

The *team* won the game.   The *staff* attended the seminar.
The *faculty* will discuss   *Management* will decide.
   the curriculum.

Team, faculty, staff, and *management* are collective nouns. When writers use collective nouns, they must remember the following rules.

Rule to Remember

1. When the **collective noun** functions as a *singular unit,* the verb that follows is *singular.*

   Examples:

   The *family is going* to the police banquet.
   (singular)
   The *jury has reached* a verdict.
   (singular)
   The *gang is* violent.
   (singular)

2. When the **collective noun** functions as *individual members,* the verb that follows is *plural.*

   Examples:

   The *family members are going* to the police banquet.
   (plural)
   The *jury members have reached* a verdict.
   (plural)
   The *members* of the gang *are violent.*
   (plural)

5. Abstract Nouns

Rule to Remember

An abstract noun identifies an idea, a belief, a feeling, or a quality.

Examples:

Justice will prevail.	*Hate* kills.
Prejudice destroys.	*Peace* is possible.

Justice, prejudice, hate, and *peace* are abstract nouns.

Exercise 1

Directions: Write concrete, proper, common, collective, or abstract to identify the noun category that classifies the following words.

Example: <u>abstract</u> pride

_____ 1. judge   _____ 6. badge

_____ 2. chief   _____ 7. Sergeant Nelson

_____ 3. officer   _____ 8. Lieutenant Gomez

_____ 4. honesty   _____ 9. team

_____ 5. inmate   _____ 10. personnel

Score = (# correct × 10) = _____%

Exercise 2

Directions: Read each sentence *carefully.* Underline the noun(s) in the following sentences.

Example: Officer <u>Nunoz</u> wrote the <u>report</u>.

1. The defendant was disappointed about the guilty verdict.

2. While searching the cell, the officer found drugs underneath the mattress.

3. The correctional officer escorted the inmate to the clinic.

4. The evidence is inadmissible in court.

5. The officer comforted the abused woman, who refused to press charges against her violent boyfriend.

6. Despite its negative publicity, Miami, Florida, is a great place to visit.

7. The officer impounded the car with the black-tinted windows.

8. The meeting will take place at 11:30 A.M. in the conference room.

9. The license plate was missing from the red van.

10. The officer arrested the juvenile for shoplifting; she stole merchandise valued at $125.

Score = (# correct × 10) = _____%

PART B

Pronouns

Rule to Remember

A pronoun acts as a substitute for the noun. The pronoun, like the noun, identifies a person, place, thing, action, quality, or belief that is being discussed. However, the pronoun is general and does not provide a specific name.

Examples: *He* stole my purse.
She ran a red light.
The chief appointed *him.*
Their testimony is important.

He, she, him, and *their* are pronouns.

Correct: *Each* officer gets *his* or *her* own patrol car.
Incorrect: *Each* officer gets *their* own patrol car.

The writer should remember the following helpful hints.

Hint 1: Singular pronouns often act as *subjects* in a sentence (I, you, he, she, and it); they are referred to as *subjective pronouns.*

Examples: *She* is a dedicated employee.
He wrote the proposal.
You are an intelligent officer.

She, he, and *you* perform the subject role.

119

Hint 2: **Plural pronouns** often act as *subjects* in a sentence (we, you, and they).

Examples: *We* are doing well in our classes at the academy.
They will graduate next week.
You will succeed if you work diligently at your studies.

We, they, and *you* perform the subject role.

Hint 3: **Singular objective pronouns** are often used as *objects* in a sentence (me, you, him, and her).

Examples: He told *me* about the robbery.
The captain asked *her* to facilitate the workshop.
The inmate told *me* about the fight.

In the first example, *he* is the subject; *me* is the object.
In the second example, *her* is the object.
In the third example, *me* is the object (not *I*).

Hint 4: **Plural objective pronouns** are often used as *objects* in a sentence (us, you, and them).

Examples: The lieutenant asked *us* a question. (not *we*)
The sergeant told *them* to leave. (not *they*)
The officer told *you* to drop the gun.

Us, them, and *you* are objects.

Exercise 1

Directions: In the following sentences, add the appropriate *subjective* or *objective* pronoun.

Example: (She, him) *She* will ask *him* for a challenging assignment.

SUBJECTIVE PRONOUN	OBJECTIVE PRONOUN
I	me
you	you
he	him
she	her
it	it
we	us
they	them

1. _____ will search the house when the warrant is ready.

2. The officer asked _____ to step out of the car.

3. _____ asked _____ for the registration to the car.

4. The chief will recommend _____ and _____.

5. You will have to ask _____ whether or not probable cause exists.

6. The officer informed _____ of my rights.

7. The witness told _____ everything about the murder.

8. _____ believe the victim's testimony.

9. The lieutenant will choose between _____ and _____.

10. _____ wants to speak to his attorney.

Score = (# correct × 10) = _____%

Exercise 2

Directions: Underline the appropriate subjective or objective pronoun.

Example: The captain complimented (he/<u>him</u>) and (I/<u>me</u>).

1. The officer asked (he/him) to step out of the cell.
2. (She/Her) showed (we/us) the contraband.
3. The officer spoke to (he/him) about the policy.
4. The lieutenant assigned (he/him) and (I/me) to the committee.
5. (She/Her) and (I/me) searched the inmate's cell.
6. Is (he/him) handling the Wallace case?
7. The sergeant told (they/them) to leave.
8. (We/Us) have a warrant for your arrest.
9. The chief recommended (he/him) and (I/me) for the position.
10. The witness told (we/us) everything (he/him) saw.

Score = (# correct × 10) = _____%

Exercise 3

Directions: Underline the appropriate subjective or objective pronoun.

Example: (<u>He</u>/Him) and (<u>I</u>/me) will be promoted.

1. (He/Him) showed (we/us) fake identification.
2. (She/Her) and (I/me) saw the suspect's car.
3. The captain named (he/him) and (I/me) to investigate the charge.
4. The witness told (we/us) about the incident.
5. The lieutenant asked (he/him) and (I/me) to follow up on the case.
6. (We/Us) believe (he/him) and (she/her).
7. (They/Them) have a warrant for (she/her) arrest.
8. (He/Him) and (I/me) will take the promotional exam.
9. (We/Us) want to speak with (they/them) about the report.
10. The sergeant informed (he/him) and (I/me) of the hearing.

Score = (# correct × 10) = _____%

PART C

Verbs

Rule to Remember

The role of a verb in a sentence is to indicate action or help make a statement. A verb is an essential part of a sentence because it gives additional information about the subject.

In addition, when a verb indicates *being* (was, is, am, were), the verb functions as a *linking* or *helping* verb.

Examples:

PRESENT TENSE	PAST TENSE	HELPING AND LINKING VERBS	
call	called	will	has
ask	asked	would	were
interview	interviewed	should	are
drive	drove	have	is
observe	observed	had	was

Action Verb Examples: She *talked* to the witness.
The judge *asked* the defendant a question.
Officer Jenkins *wrote* an excellent report.

Helping and Linking Verb Examples: She *is* talking to the witness.
The judge *was* asking the defendant a question.
Officer Jenkins *is* head of this group.

Exercise 1

Directions: In the following sentences, underline the verb(s).

Example: The inmate <u>met</u> with his attorney.

1. The officer arrested the suspect.
2. During the robbery, Mr. Adams assaulted Mr. Taylor.
3. The driver struck the pedestrian.
4. The meeting will be held at noon.
5. The department will close early for the holidays.
6. Stop! (*Hint:* The subject is *you.*)
7. The major eats a well-balanced lunch.
8. The sergeant reviews the reports.
9. If you have any questions, ask your supervisor.
10. The inmate wrote a book about his experiences in prison.

Score = (# correct × 10) = _____%

PART D

Adjectives

Rules to Remember

The adjective's purpose in a sentence is to describe a noun or pronoun.

An adjective often answers the following questions:

How much?   **Which one?**
What kind?   **How many?**

The words *a, an,* and *the* in a sentence are in a different category of adjectives called *articles.*

Examples: *Five* guns are missing from the *metal* box.
How many guns are missing? *Five.*
From which box? The *metal* one.

The blue Porsche was stolen.
Which Porsche? The *blue* one.
The is the article.

The tall, thin, brunette woman robbed the bank.
Which woman? The *tall, thin, brunette* one.
The is the article.

Exercise 1

Directions: In the following sentences, underline the adjectives.

Example: The <u>frightened</u> child did not want to speak to the <u>concerned</u> officer.

1. The suspect told the officers several different stories about his involvement in the tragic homicide.

2. The woman wearing a red T-shirt and blue shorts stole a video from the store.

3. Some criminologists believe that delinquent behavior is learned.

4. Dedicated trainees usually do well in their difficult classes.

5. The four hostile juveniles screamed obscenities at the officers.

6. Some inmates adapt well to the confined environment.

7. Many parolees abide by the fair conditions set by their parole officer.

8. Educational programs and vocational training are offered in some prisons.

9. The brand-new computer performs many necessary functions.

10. The brown Dodge, with the broken headlight, is missing a license plate.

Score = (# correct × 10) = _____%

Comparisons

Adjectives are often used to *compare* the degree of something.

Example: smart

Positive	Jim is a *smart* officer.
Comparative	Jim is *smarter* than Bob.
Superlative	Jim is the *smartest* officer I know.

Example: slow

Positive	His car is *slow*.
Comparative	His car is *slower* than my car.
Superlative	His car is the *slowest* car in the lot.

Rule to Remember

The writer should note that adding **-er** or **-est** allows for comparisons to be made. However, adding *-er* or *-est* is not always appropriate or correct. Sometimes, *more, most, less,* or *least* should come before the adjective.

Example: <u>difficult</u>

Positive	The promotional exam is *difficult.*
Comparative	The promotional exam is *more difficult* than the entry exam.
Superlative	The promotional exam is the *most difficult* exam I have ever taken.

Example: <u>athletic</u>

Positive	Greg is not *athletic.*
Comparative	Greg is *less athletic* than Mark.
Superlative	Greg is the *least athletic* friend of mine.

Exercise 2

Directions: Write three sentences for each word using the positive, comparative, and superlative forms.

Example:

Positive	a. Syd is a *dedicated* officer.
Comparative	b. Syd is *more dedicated* than Steve.
Superlative	c. Syd is the *most dedicate* officer in the department.

1. fast

   a. _____

   b. _____

   c. _____

2. good

   a. _____

   b. _____

   c. _____

3. bad

a. _____

b. _____

c. _____

4. strong

a. _____

b. _____

c. _____

5. challenging

a. _____

b. _____

c. _____

6. pleasurable

a. _____

b. _____

c. _____

7. rough

a. _____

b. _____

c. _____

8. stubborn

a. _____

b. _____

c. _____

PART E

Adverbs

Rules to Remember

The role of the adverb in a sentence is to describe a verb, adverb, or adjective. Often the adverb answers the following questions:

When?
Where?
How?

Adverbs commonly (not always) end in **ly**.

Examples: The chief will be leaving *early*.

Question: *When* will the chief be leaving?
Answer: *early*

The witness is *outside* near the steps.

Question: *Where* is the witness?
Answer: *outside*

The suspect walked *slowly* away from the car.

Question: *How* did the suspect walk?
Answer: *slowly*

Exercise 1

Directions: Underline the adverb(s) in the following sentences.

Example: The victim screamed <u>loudly</u> when she saw the defendant.

1. Sometimes witnesses who appear in court lie about the facts of a case.

2. Officer Davison is highly respected by his colleagues.

3. The defendant spoke quickly when he gave his deposition.

4. Sergeant Sherman will be leaving immediately after the seminar.

5. The burglary took place at approximately 1300 hours.

6. Officer Carter proofreads her reports carefully.

7. The juvenile's mother prayed quietly for her son to be found innocent.

8. Now is the time to become familiar with the rules of writing.

9. The inmate stormed angrily into his cell.

10. The woman talked bitterly about her demanding landlord.

Score = (# correct × 10) = _____%

PART F

Prepositions

Rules to Remember

The preposition's purpose in a sentence is to show the link between a noun or pronoun and other words in the sentence.

A prepositional phrase, such as *with a warrant,* cannot stand alone. Other words in addition to the prepositional phrase must exist to make the statement complete.

Let's make the phrase *with a warrant* into a complete sentence.

a. Before an officer can search a home, she or he must present the homeowner *with a warrant.*

or

b. *With a warrant,* a police officer can lawfully search a suspect's home.

or

c. A police officer *with a warrant* can lawfully search a suspect's home.

The following words are prepositions:

about	before	except	since
above	behind	from	through
across	beside	in	toward
against	beyond	like	under
along	during	onto	up

Exercise 1

Directions: Select the appropriate preposition from the word list on page 131 for the following sentences.

Example: The meeting is <u>about</u> to begin.

1. The robber stashed the money _____ the mattress.

2. The burglar entered the home _____ an open window.

3. Remind me to call the lieutenant _____ I leave home.

4. The intruder was hiding _____ the front door.

5. The juvenile ran _____ the yard.

6. The body was found _____ the road.

7. The inmate was locked up _____ his will.

8. _____ the trial, the defendant whispered to her attorney.

9. Burns was denied bail _____ he has a history of prior arrests.

10. The judge wants to speak to you _____ your client.

11. _____ ten minutes, the chief will address the panel.

12. The perpetrator holding a knife ran _____ me.

13. The officer chased the felon _____ a flight of stairs.

14. The driver, traveling eighty miles an hour, was driving _____ the speed limit.

15. The correctional officer walked _____ the waxed floors of the jail.

16. The stubborn drug addict is _____ help.

17. All of the sergeants will be at the meeting _____ Sergeant Wilson.

18. The drunk driver drove her car _____ the sidewalk.

19. The officer looks _____ his father.

20. _____ now on, I will proofread my reports.

Score = (# correct × 5) = _____%

PART G

Conjunctions

Rule to Remember

A conjunction's role in a sentence is to connect words with other words, clauses, and ideas. A quick way to remember conjunctions is with the FANBOYS acronym. Writers of reports often use the following conjunctions:

F = for
A = and
N = nor
B = but
O = or
Y = yet
S = so

These seven conjunctions are necessary to join two main clauses. When using a conjunction with *two complete sentences,* you should place a comma before the conjunction.

Examples   The officer arrested the suspect, *and* he read him
the Miranda warnings.
The officer arrested the suspect, *but* he forgot to
read him the Miranda warnings.
You should work hard today, *or* you will suffer the
consequences tomorrow.

Examples   Incorrect: Jogging is tiring, and invigorating.
Correct: Jogging is tiring and invigorating.

Incorrect: The inmate is hungry, and cold.
Correct: The inmate is hungry and cold.

Exercise 1

Directions: Write a sentence using each of the following conjunctions once.

Example: I wrote the report, but I did not sign it.

1. and   5. or
2. but   6. so
3. for   7. yet
4. nor

1. _____
2. _____
3. _____
4. _____
5. _____
6. _____
7. _____

PART H

Interjections

Rule to Remember

An interjection's purpose in a sentence is to express emotion.

Examples:
   a. *Wow!* I got the job!
   b. *Hey!* He stole my purse!
   c. *Help!* (The subject is *You.*)

Exercise 1

Directions: Write a sentence using each of the following interjections once.

Example: duck *Duck!* He's got a gun!

1. Oh	6. Hey
2. Stop	7. No
3. Police	8. Yes
4. Freeze	9. Wait
5. Move	10. Help

1. _____

2. _____

3. _____

4. _____

5. _____

6. _____

7. _____

8. _____

9. _____

10. _____

Final Note

In the introduction, I mentioned that each word serves a unique function in a sentence. However, sometimes changing the form of a word to use in a sentence makes the word a different part of speech.

Example: a. belief
                  b. believes
                  c. believable

    a. He has a strong *belief* about capital punishment. (noun)
    b. He *believes* that inmates should be rehabilitated. (verb)
    c. He is a *believable* witness for the prosecution. (adjective)

Exercise 1

Directions: Use each word in a sentence.

1. well (noun)   _____

    well (adverb)   _____

2. relief (noun)   _____

    relieve (verb)   _____

3. one (adjective) _____

    one (noun)   _____

4. challenge (noun) _____

    challenge (verb) _____

5. report (noun)   _____

    report (verb)   _____

Exercise 2

Directions: Answer each question and provide an example for the underlined word.

1. **Q.** What is the purpose of a <u>noun</u> in a sentence?

A. _____

Example: _____

2. **Q.** What is the purpose of a <u>pronoun</u> in a sentence?

A. _____

Example: _____

3. **Q.** What is the purpose of a <u>verb</u> in a sentence?

A. _____

Example: _____

4. **Q.** What is the purpose of an <u>adjective</u> in a sentence?

A. _____

Example: _____

5. **Q.** What is the purpose of an <u>adverb</u> in a sentence?

A. _____

Example: _____

6. **Q.** What is the purpose of a <u>preposition</u> in a sentence?

A. _____

Example: _____

7. **Q.** What is the purpose of a <u>conjunction</u> in a sentence?

A. _____

Example: _____

8. **Q.** What is the purpose of an <u>interjection</u> in a sentence?

A. _____

Example: _____

Exercise 3

Directions: Identify the part of speech for each underlined word.

Noun	**Adverb**
Pronoun	**Preposition**
Verb	**Conjunction**
Adjective	**Interjection**

_____ I was patrolling the South Miami <u>area</u> when I spotted the suspect's car: a 1987 blue Chevrolet Camero. _____ I <u>asked</u> the dispatcher to check the tag (XYZ 123), and she told me the car was stolen. _____ When I asked the driver to step out of the car, he hesitated <u>momentarily</u>. _____ When he stepped out of the car, I frisked him according to the standards of <u>Terry vs. Ohio</u>.

_____ Each of his pockets <u>contained</u> 4 milligrams paraphernalia. _____ Specifically, I found what appeared to be a bag of marijuana in his right pocket <u>and</u> a suspected crack-cocaine rock in his left pocket. _____ The <u>suspect</u> asked Officer Smith and me if he was under arrest. _____We said, "<u>Yes!</u>" _____ I arrested the <u>suspect</u>. _____ I read <u>him</u> the Miranda warnings from my card. _____ I <u>called</u> the dispatcher who said I could go to lunch. _____ When I <u>turned</u> east, I spotted the fugitive's car.

SECTION III

Homophones

Rule to Remember

Homophones and problem words or troublesome words are words that are similar in sound but different in spelling and meaning.

Directions: Read the word lists and definitions in the following three parts. Identify the appropriate word for each sentence in the exercises following each part.

Part A

a	used with *consonant* sounds
an	used with *vowel* sounds
accept	to receive; to make a favorable response to
except	with the exclusion or exception of
access	admission; entry to
excess	exceeding a limit; overabundance
adapt	to become accustomed to; adjust
adept	skillful; good at
adopt	to select; choose
addition	added part
edition	version of
advice	instruction; guidance (n)
advise	to inform; to counsel (v)
affect	involve; impact
effect	to produce; to cause
agree to	agree to a thing
agree with	agree with a person
aisle	passageway; avenue
isle	island

139

allowed	granted permission
aloud	out loud; using the voice
all ready	everything or everybody is ready
already	previously; beforehand
all together	everyone or as a group
altogether	without exception; completely
altar	place of worship
alter	to change
all ways	every approach
always	every time
among	refers to *three* or *more* people or things
between	refers to *two* people or things
bare	naked; lacking cover
bear	to carry; animal
brake	a device for stopping or slowing
break	separate; shatter into parts
breath	air taken into lungs
breathe	to inhale and exhale air
bring	carry with
take	get into one's possession; grasp accumulated goods
capital	finances; city; types of letter (a)
capitol	government building
cease	to stop or discontinue
seize	to take
cite	to quote or refer to
sight	vision
site	location
coarse	rough texture
course	plan; class
choose	to select; single out
chose	past tense of the verb *choose*
complement	counterpart; accompaniment
compliment	to praise (v); expression of admiration (n)
confidant	close friend
confident	certain
credential	reference; something that gives credit or confidence
credible	believable
creditable	deserving of praise

deposition	statement taken under oath
disposition	personality; character; outcome of a court case
desert	abandon; leave
dessert	a sweet served at the end of a meal

Exercise 1

Directions: After you have read the preceding word list and definitions, underline the appropriate word in parentheses in each sentence.

1. (A, An) citizen wrote a letter of commendation to Officer Brown.

2. (A, An) opportunity like this does not happen every day.

3. Everyone is going to the baseball game (accept, except) Officer Fuentes.

4. Officer Johnson will (accept, except) the promotion.

5. The suspect drove in (access, excess) of eighty-five miles per hour.

6. The bank employee had (access, excess) to the vault.

7. An inmate must (adapt, adept, adopt) to the prison environment.

8. He is (adapt, adept, adopt) at athletic activities.

9. The captain has (adapted, adepted, adopted) the sergeant's proposal.

10. The lieutenant gave the new recruits (advice, advise) on how to handle stress.

11. I (advice, advise) you to speak to an attorney.

12. Motivated supervisors (affect, effect) similar results in their employees.

13. Will the change in management (affect, effect) our department?

14. The captain will (agree to, agree with) the chief that more promotions should be given.

15. The chief will (agree to, agree with) the new budget being proposed for the upcoming year.

16. The officer chased the juvenile down the supermarket (aisle, isle).

17. The officials captured the fugitive on an (aisle, isle) near Bermuda.

18. Inmate Smith is (allowed, aloud) to communicate with her attorney.

19. Every morning, Inmate Smith sings (allowed, aloud) in the shower.

20. The major (all ready, already) spoke with the group about tardiness.

21. The recruits are (all ready, already) to begin their careers in law enforcement.

22. The narcotics investigators were (all together, altogether) in the van.

23. (All together, Altogether), 200 marijuana plants are missing.

24. At the (altar, alter), the officers exchanged their marital vows.

25. During the trial, the witness tried to (altar, alter) her original statement.

26. Officer Sutton (all ways, always) writes excellent reports.

27. Before she makes a final decision, the captain explores (all ways, always) of doing things.

28. The decision to plea-bargain is (among, between) the prosecutor and the defense attorney.

29. The fight was (among, between) four juveniles who are all under the age of eighteen.

30. According to the Second Amendment, citizens have the right to (bare, bear) arms.

31. The inmate's cell looked (bare, bear).

32. The juvenile's violent temper caused him to (brake, break) his mother's vase.

33. The mechanic replaced the (brakes, breaks) on the patrol car.

34. (Bring, Take) me the arrest report.

35. (Bring, Take) the evidence to the lab when you leave.

36. The (capital, capitol) of Florida is Tallahassee.

37. The officers patrolled the (capital, capitol) building in Washington, D.C.

38. "(Cease, Seize) your drug activity," said Officer Michaels.

39. The officer (ceased, seized) fifty pounds of cocaine from the trunk of the defendant's car.

40. The (cite, sight, site) of the new prison will be near the airport.

41. My eye (cite, sight, site) is slowly getting worse as I get older.

42. MI officer must (cite, sight, site) the appropriate statute on the attest report.

43. Officer Brown signed up for a criminology (coarse, course) at the college.

44. Officer Miller had to retrieve the weapon from the (coarse, course) shrubs.

45. The captain will (choose, chose) the officer who deserves the promotion.

46. He (choose, chose) Officer Raskin.

47. The sergeant (complemented, complimented) Officer Henderson during the meeting.

48. Apple pie is a nice (complement, compliment) to any meal.

49. Officer Nelson's display of leadership and dedication to the law enforcement profession is (credential, credible, creditable).

50. Because Officer Black has outstanding (credentials, credibles, creditables), she was honored at the awards ceremony.

51. Ms. Diaz made a (credential, credible, creditable) witness for the prosecution.

52. Officer White gave his (deposition, disposition) at the state attorney's office.

53. The defendant appears to have a hostile (deposition, disposition).

54. Mr. Smith left the restaurant without paying for his (desert, dessert).

55. Ms. Daniels stole a car to commit a robbery; then she (deserted, desserted) the car near the highway.

Part B

device	gadget; instrument
devise	to plot
disinterested	unbiased
uninterested	not interested in
elicit	to draw out
illicit	unlawful
eligible	worthy choice; qualified
illegible	not legible; unclear writing
eminent	respected; outstanding
imminent	likely to occur
every day	each separate day
everyday	common; ordinary
every body	each separate body
everybody	everyone
farther	beyond; relates to physical distance
further	additional; more
fewer	small quantity or number of something that can be counted
less	more limited amount; applies to something that cannot be counted

formally	properly
formerly	previously
forth	ahead
fourth	number in a series
hear	listen
here	location
heard	past tense of the verb *hear*
herd	a crowd; to drive livestock
hours	time
ours	ownership by two or more people
imply	to introduce an idea; to suggest
infer	to reach a conclusion
instance	case; example
instant	refers to time; a moment in time
inter	(prefix) between
intra	(prefix) within
its	shows ownership
it's	contraction of *it is*
knew	had knowledge of; past tense of the verb *know*
new	recent
lead	front position (a); to go in advance (v); metal (n)
led	past tense of the verb *lead*
liable	to be responsible for
libel	false publication
lie	to be untruthful; to recline
lay	to place
loose	not tightly bound
lose	to fail to win
loss	something destroyed (n)
might of	incorrect form
might have	correct form
one	number
won	past tense of the verb *win*
passed	past tense of the verb *pass*
past	time gone by (x); former (a); after or beyond (prep); go beyond a joint (adv)
patience	the quality of being patient
patients	those under medical treatment
peace	calm
piece	a part of

pear	edible fruit
pair	two persons or items; couple
pare	to cut back; reduce

perspective	point of view
prospective	likely; expected

Exercise 2

Directions: After you have read the preceding word list and definitions, underline the appropriate word in parentheses in each sentence.

1. The burglar (deviced, devised) an ingenious method of entering the home.

2. An officer's radio is a (device, devise) that may save his or her life.

3. The mediator is the (disinterested, uninterested) party who helps citizens resolve their disputes.

4. She seemed (disinterested, uninterested) in the outcome of the case.

5. The narcotics investigators tried to (elicit, illicit) a response from the drug dealer.

6. The defendant was incarcerated for participating in (elicit, illicit) conduct.

7. The inmate is (eligible, illegible) for parole next year.

8. The juvenile's handwriting is (eligible, illegible).

9. The fugitive's capture is (eminent, imminent).

10. Corporal Washington is an (eminent, imminent) correctional representative.

11. (Every day, Everyday) last week, a burglary took place at 0400 hours.

12. Crime, unfortunately, is an (every day, everyday) occurrence in our city.

13. (Every body, Everybody) who was found by the investigators had been badly beaten.

14. (Every body, Everybody) is invited to the communications conference.

15. The police station is (farther, further) than the jail.

16. "Mrs. Jones, if you have any (farther, further) questions, please call," said Detective Matthews.

17. Overall, there are (fewer, less) robberies this year than last year.

18. As I get older, I seem to have (fewer, less) patience with people.

19. He (formally, formerly) attended night classes at the college.

20. The chief will (formally, formerly) introduce his successor at the meeting.

21. According to the (Forth, Fourth) Amendment, individuals have the right to be protected against unlawful searches and seizures.

22. Officer Garcia said, "Step (forth, fourth) with your hands up."

23. The juror did not (hear, here) the judge's instructions.

24. The officer found the weapon (hear, here).

25. Ms. Thomas told the officers she (heard, herd) a chilling scream.

26. The jury deliberated the case for six (hours, ours).

27. The motorcycle with the black seat is (hours, ours).

28. Mrs. Jones (implied, inferred) that she knew something about the murder.

29. The investigators (implied, inferred) that Mrs. Jones committed the murder.

30. In almost every (instance, instants) of automobile-related death, drivers did not wear their seat belts.

31. In an (instance, instant), the driver of the car hit the tree.

32. The (inter, intra)state highways merge near Altanta, Georgia.

33. The Florida (inter, intra)state highway is always congested during rush hour.

34. (Its, It's) very sad that Officer Wilson was hurt during the armed robbery.

35. The bird built (its, it's) nest near the inmate's window.

36. I (knew, new) Officer Margolis when we were kids in elementary school.

37. The (knew, new) police cars are faster than the old cars.

38. Trainee Joseph (leads, lead) the class in academic rank.

39. Officer Jones (lead, led) the inmate to the clinic.

40. The driver of the car is (liable, libel) for the victim's damages.

41. The chief is suing the editor of the newspaper for (liable, libel).

42. I will (lie, lay) the report on your desk so you can proofread it.

43. The defendant told a (lie, lay) while he was under oath.

44. After she lost ten pounds, Officer Carmello's uniform was (loose, lose, loss) in the waist.

45. If we do not study, we will (loose, lose, loss) our high average.

46. The (loose, lose, loss) of property is not as tragic as the (loose, lose, loss) of life.

47. The trainee (might of, might have) passed the exam if he had worked harder.

48. (One, Won) trainee with leadership qualities can motivate the rest of the group.

49. The Dolphins (one, won) the game last week.

50. The driver of the Ferrari was traveling ninety miles per hour when she (passed, past) the police car.

51. Today's graduation reminds me of a (passed, past) ceremony.

52. "(Patience, Patients) is a virtue."

53. After the hurricane, many (patience, patients) needed extra care.

54. The rival gangs decided to make (peace, piece) before the new year.

55. The inmate ate a (peace, piece) of the pie.

56. Officer Sanchez ate a (pear, pair, pare) with her lunch.

57. I always keep an extra (pear, pair, pare) of scissors in my desk drawer.

58. Due to financial problems, the company decided to (pear, pair, pare) down the number of its employees.

59. The attorney has an interesting (perspective, prospective) about the case.

60. The (perspective, prospective) candidate has a good chance of winning the election.

Part C

personal	secret; confidential
personnel	staff
plain	ordinary
plane	airplane
precede	to come before
proceed	to move ahead
precedence	seniority; priority
precedent	classic example; rule of law used in similar cases
presence	the condition of being present
presents	gifts
principal	individual in control (m); primary as main (a)
principle	basic rule
quiet	silent
quite	entirely; completely
quit	to discontinue; stop
red	color
read	present and past tense of the verb *read*

set	to place; to put into position
sit	to be seated
speak to	to tell (*involves two people*)
speak with	to discuss (*involves three or more people*)
stationary	unmoving; motionless
stationery	writing material, paper, and envelopes
statue	sculpture
statute	law enacted by the legislature
tenant	an inhabitant
tenet	principle
than	used to compare
then	next in time
their	possessive case of *they*
there	in that place
they're	contraction of *they are*
thorough	complete; detailed
threw	past tense of the verb *throw*
through	in one side and out the other
to	in a direction toward
too	so; also
two	number
trustee	member of a board of directors
trusty	an inmate who is given special privileges
use to	incorrect form; past tense of the verb *to be*
used to	correct form; past tense of the verb *to be accustomed to*
wait	to remain; to delay
weight	volume; heaviness
weak	frail; lacking strength
week	seven-day period
weather	condition of atmosphere
whether	if it is so
wither	fade; to lose strength
who	which person, used as the subject in a sentence
whom	which person, used as the object in a sentence
who's	contraction of *who is*
whose	shows ownership
your	shows ownership
you're	contraction of *you are*

Exercise 3

Directions: After you have read the preceding word list and definitions, underline the appropriate word in parentheses in each sentence.

1. The (personal, personnel) of the correctional facility are dedicated and ethical.

2. The inmate is writing a book about his (personal, personnel) struggle with drug abuse.

3. 1 like to travel by (plain, plane).

4. The new house looked (plain, plane) without any furniture.

5. The Fourth Amendment (precedes, proceeds) the Fifth Amendment.

6. The sergeant told us to (precede, proceed) with the investigation.

7. Family obligations should take (precedence, precedent) over hobbies.

8. The *Kent* ruling set a (precedence, precedent) for future juvenile court cases.

9. The (presence, presents) of his wife helped the victim cope with the difficult trial.

10. The officer brought (presence, presents) to the sick children at the hospital.

11. The (principal, principle) met with the officer before the start of the DARE presentation.

12. Sometimes (principal, principle) must not be compromised.

13. The suspect was (quiet, quite, quit) during the drive to the jail.

14. The drug addict is trying to (quiet, quite, quit) her unhealthy abuse of pills.

15. The officer was (quiet, quite, quit) relieved that the crowd was pleasant.

16. Officers should (red, read) Miranda warnings from a card.

17. The suspect was driving a (red, read) Toyota when the officer pulled him over for reckless driving.

18. The officer (set, sit) her gun on the table.

19. "Please (set, sit) down, Mr. Smith," said the attorney.

20. The captain wants to (speak to, speak with) you about your tardiness.

21. The officer will (speak to, speak with) the students about handgun safety.

22. During his lunch hour, the officer relieves stress by riding a (stationary, stationery) bicycle.

23. The police department's new (stationary, stationery) is very impressive.

24. Legislators are responsible for enacting (statues, statutes).

25. To honor the retired chief, the department will display a (statue, statute) of its fine leader.

26. When the (tenant, tenet) refused to pay rent, the landlord called the police.

27. The (tenant, tenet) of the group is explained in the pamphlet.

28. The victim's temper is worse (than, then) the defendant's.

29. First, the suspect ran a red light; (than, then) she struck a pedestrian.

30. (Their, There, They're) excuse is hard to believe.

31. The suspect tossed the gun over (their, there, they're).

32. (Their, There, They're) going to the preliminary hearing at 0900 hours.

33. The violent juvenile (thorough, threw, through) a glass bowl at his sister.

34. The burglar climbed (thorough, threw, through) an open window.

35. The officer conducted a (thorough, threw, through) search of the suspect's home.

36. The convicted drug dealer will go (to, too, two) prison for (to, too, two) years.

37. I, (to, too, two), am proud of you.

38. The (trustee, trusty) at the prison will be released on parole.

39. The (trustee, trusty) at the college has issued raises for all employees.

40. The officer is having a difficult time getting (used to, use to) the evening schedule.

41. Officer Williams had to (wait, weight) twenty minutes for the juvenile's dad to arrive.

42. Officer Monroe lost a lot of (wait, weight) while she was on vacation.

43. The (weak, week) individuals quit; however, the strong-minded individuals survive.

44. The (weak, week) passes quickly when a person is busy working.

45. Letter carriers perform their duties regardless of the (weather, whether, wither).

46. (Weather, Whether, Wither) you think so or not, violent crime is on the rise.

47. The elderly man looked (weathered, whethered, withered) and frail.

48. (Who, Whom) is responsible for the damage?

49. (Who, Whom) did the victim identify in the lineup?

50. (Who's, Whose) car is double-parked on the street?

51. (Who's, Whose) the owner of the car?

52. (Your, You're) hard work and dedication will pay off.

53. (Your, You're) a credit to the criminal justice field.

SECTION IV

The Sentence

PART A

What Is a Sentence?

Rule to Remember

Question: What is a sentence?

Answer: **A sentence is a group of words that contains a subject and a verb. A sentence expresses a complete thought. A fragment does not express a complete thought and lacks a subject and/or verb. A fragment is incomplete.**

Examples:
1. <u>Fragment</u>   Is a dedicated professional.
2. <u>Fragment</u>   Officer Martin a dedicated professional.
3. <u>Sentence</u>   Officer Martin is a dedicated professional.

1. This statement is incomplete. These words are missing a subject. The reader must ask, "Who is a dedicated professional?"
2. This statement is incomplete. These words are missing a verb.
3. Hooray! Now we have a complete sentence that contains a subject and a verb.

Please remember that during the note-taking stage of writing a report, you can write in a "choppy" manner if you desire. However, when you write the actual report, you must write in complete sentences.

Exercise 1

Directions: On the blank provided, identify the following as C for complete sentence or F for fragment.

_____ 1. Because the suspect ran a red light.

_____ 2. Officer Lee received a promotion.

_____ 3. Tomorrow I will take the report-writing exam.

_____ 4. Although writing skills are important.

_____ 5. Grabbed her purse.

_____ 6. Officer Wilson left.

_____ 7. Worked late last night.

_____ 8. In the beginning.

_____ 9. Hard work pays off.

_____ 10. Found paraphernalia in the cell.

Score = (# correct × 10) = _____ %

Exercise 2

Directions: On the blank provided, identify the following as C for complete sentence or F for fragment.

_____ 1. Searched the trunk.

_____ 2. The officer questioned the witness.

_____ 3. The suspect stopped running.

_____ 4. Drinking for three hours.

_____ 5. During the meeting.

_____ 6. Because it's a holiday.

_____ 7. Along with the others.

_____ 8. Officer Lawson found guns in the trunk.

_____ 9. Since you study hard.

_____ 10. Write the report.

Score = (# correct × 10) = _____ %

Exercise 3

Directions: On the blank provided, identify the following as C for complete sentence or F for fragment.

_____ 1. We saluted.

_____ 2. Watch the suspect.

_____ 3. After the robbery.

_____ 4. Found a shank in the cell.

_____ 5. Smoking marijuana in the yard.

_____ 6. I was dispatched to Park Drive.

_____ 7. Questioned the witness.

_____ 8. I confiscated four weapons.

_____ 9. He signed the incident report.

_____ 10. She wrote the memorandum.

Score = (# correct × 10) = _____ %

Exercise 4

Directions: On the blank provided, identify the following as C for complete sentence or F for fragment.

_____ 1. Jones committed the assault.

_____ 2. Committed the burglary.

_____ 3. We questioned them.

_____ 4. Search the house.

_____ 5. Arrest him.

_____ 6. Without a warrant.

_____ 7. Report to the meeting.

_____ 8. Officer Smith in the other room.

_____ 9. The juvenile fled.

_____ 10. She wrote the report.

Score = (# correct × 10) = _____ %

PART B

Changing Fragments to Sentences

Rule to Remember

To make a fragment into a sentence:

1. Decide whether the group of words lacks a subject or a verb.
2. If it lacks one or the other, add what it needs and complete the thought.
3. Sometimes a fragment can have both a subject and a verb but have an incomplete thought that leaves the reader hanging; in this case, finish the thought.

Examples:

Incorrect: The weapon used during the robbery.

Correct: The officer found *the weapon used during the robbery.*
The suspect *used the weapon during the robbery.*

Exercise 1

Directions: The following groups of words are fragments (incomplete thoughts). Rewrite each fragment as a complete sentence.

1. Those juveniles by the window.

   _____

2. When the officer saw the suspect's car.

   _____

3. Which has a flat tire.

   _____

4. During the trial.

   _____

5. Like a professional.

   _____

6. At the defendant's home.

   _____

7. On January 31, the defendant.

   _____

8. While stopped at a red light.

   _____

9. Without probable cause.

   _____

10. Allowed to search.

    _____

Score = (# correct × 10) = _____ %

Exercise 2

Directions: Rewrite each fragment as a complete sentence.

1. Searched the car.

   _____

2. The new drill sergeant.

   _____

3. In the cafeteria.

   _____

4. Almost got away.

   _____

5. Has a search warrant.

   _____

6. After the clerk read the verdict.

   _____

7. Called 911.

   _____

8. Drove eighty miles per hour.

   _____

9. Had a gun.

   _____

10. Took the merchandise.

   _____

Score = (# correct × 10) = _____%

Exercise 3

Directions: Rewrite each fragment as a complete sentence.

1. That can issue a search warrant.

   _____

2. Addresses the importance of constitutional rights.

   _____

3. When force is justified.

   _____

4. Reasonable grounds to believe.

   _____

5. Is incarcerated in a maximum-security facility.

   _____

6. May be seized.

   _____

7. Incident to a lawful arrest.

   _____

8. Acted in good faith.

   _____

9. Unlocked the trunk of the van.

   _____

10. Transported the suspects to the station.

   _____

Score = (# correct × 10) = _____%

PART C

Misplaced Phrases

Rule to Remember

A professional officer is responsible for presenting written facts in a clear, concise, and accurate manner. When you misplace phrases, your writing appears comical and foolish. When you misplace phrases, your credibility plummets. Can you afford that?

Let's evaluate the following statement:

While I was patrolling the downtown area, I left my squad car behind Donny's Diner, which ran out of gas.

Question: What ran out of gas?
Answer: According to what the officer wrote, the reader must conclude that Donny's Diner ran out of gas.

Let's revise this statement.

Option 1: While I was patrolling the downtown area, I left my squad car, which ran out of gas, behind Donny's Diner.

OR

Option 2: While I was patrolling the downtown area, my squad car ran out of gas. I left the car behind Donny's Diner.

OR

Option 3: My squad car ran out of gas while I was patrolling the downtown area. Therefore, I left the car behind Donny's Diner.

OR

Option 4: Because my squad car ran out of gas while I was patrolling the downtown area, I left the car behind Donny's Diner.

All four options are *clear, concise,* and *accurate.* Now it's your turn.

Exercise 1

Directions: The following sentences contain misplaced phrases. Revise these sentences to read in a clear, concise, and accurate manner.

Example:

Dressed in yellow ballet outfits, the officers questioned the girls.

The officers questioned the girls who were dressed in yellow ballet outfits.

1. I saw five kilograms of cocaine walking down Palm Avenue.

   _____

   _____

2. While waiting in line for fifteen minutes, Inmate Murphy's cereal turned soggy.

   _____

   _____

3. Officer Miller drove to the convenience store exhausted from the chase.

   _____

   _____

4. Preparing for the state exam, Trainee Smith's outlines provided valuable information.

   _____

   _____

5. Leaving the window open, Tony's stereo was taken.

   _____

   _____

6. Major O'Hara ate a roast beef sandwich on the bench with Swiss cheese.

   _____

   _____

7. The officer found it difficult to chase the suspect wearing a tight uniform.

   _____

   _____

8. The patrol cars were parked in the lot with Florida license plates.

   _____

   _____

9. The defendant dropped a plastic bag to the ground retrieved by this officer.

_____

_____

10. Sergeant Barnett always reads the reports wearing glasses.

_____

_____

Exercise 2

Directions: The following sentences contain misplaced phrases. Revise these sentences to read in a clear, concise, and accurate manner.

Example:

The search warrant is on the captain's desk, which has been signed.

The signed search warrant is on the captain's desk.

1. Up in December again, the chief was troubled by the number of reported robberies.

_____

_____

2. The computer is in Lieutenant Nelson's office, which is broken.

_____

_____

3. When he responded to a domestic violence call, a dog attacked Officer Weber.

_____

_____

4. I looked out the window and saw the inmates in the yard with a crack.

_____

_____

5. I purchased a Smith & Wesson from the dealer without a trigger.

_____

_____

6. The officer ate a ham sandwich at the cafeteria that was rotten.

_____

_____

7. Officer Scum could see the fire driving down the street.

_____

_____

8. The juvenile smashed the glass bowl with bare fists.

_____

_____

9. The arrest report is on the sergeant's desk, which is well written.

_____

_____

10. The supply closet contains uniforms with a squeaky door.

_____

_____

Score = (# correct × 10) = _____%

PART D

Run-on Sentence (Fused Sentence)

Rule to Remember

A run-on or fused sentence allows two sentences to run together without proper punctuation and/or coordinating conjunctions (*for, and, nor, but, or, yet, so*).

The run-on sentence does not indicate a break or pause in thought.

The run-on sentence can be corrected by:

1. Inserting a period and writing two separate sentences
2. Inserting a semicolon
3. Inserting a comma and a coordinating conjunction
4. Revising one part of the fragment as a dependent clause of a complete sentence

Example:

Incorrect:	The defendant started screaming during the trial the judge asked him to stop.
Option 1:	The defendant started screaming during the trial. The judge asked him to stop.

OR

Option 2:	The defendant started screaming during the trial; therefore, the judge asked him to stop.

OR

Option 3:	The defendant started screaming during the trial, so the judge asked him to stop.

OR

Option 4:	When the defendant started screaming during the trial, the judge asked him to stop.

Exercise 1

Directions: Correct each run-on sentence by using one of the four types of correction.

1. The officer searched the suspect's home without a warrant therefore the evidence was inadmissible in court.

   _____

   _____

2. The correctional officer found cocaine in the inmate's cell therefore the inmate's privileges were taken away.

   _____

   _____

3. The defendant waived his right to an attorney then the officer started to question him.

   _____

   _____

4. Crime is escalating across the state therefore the governor wants to hire more law enforcement officers.

   _____

   _____

5. Conflicts will often arise at the workplace therefore individuals must communicate their feelings in a positive manner.

   _____

   _____

6. Some juveniles make inappropriate decisions regarding drug use therefore adults must offer guidance and support.

   _____

   _____

7. Prisons across the country are overcrowded thus inmates are being released early.

   _____

   _____

8. The law enforcement field can be stressful therefore individuals must find ways to manage stress.

   _____

   _____

9. Some victims are terrified when they appear in court however others are very calm.

   _____

   _____

10. The witness was the only person who saw what happened unfortunately he claimed to have seen nothing.

_____

_____

Score = (# correct × 10) = _____%

Exercise 2

Directions: Correct each run-on sentence by using one of the four types of correction suggestions.

1. Reports should be accurate therefore one must record answers to basic questions.

_____

_____

2. Reports should be legible thus one should print in capital letters.

_____

_____

3. Reports should be concise however many writers neglect this rule.

_____

_____

4. Reports should be factual therefore the officer should not express his or her opinion.

_____

_____

5. Reports should be written in a clear manner unfortunately some writers use jargon and slang.

_____

_____

6. Notes should be recorded in a notebook therefore you should purchase one today.

_____

_____

7. You should not write reports in the passive voice therefore you should practice writing in the active voice.

_____

_____

8. Write reports in the first person however some officers write in the third person.

   _____

   _____

9. Supervisors evaluate your reports therefore you should proof-read reports before turning them in.

   _____

   _____

10. Reports should be complete therefore make sure all boxes are filled in appropriately.

    _____

    _____

Score = (# correct × 10) = _____%

PART E

Subject Identification

Rule to Remember

A complete sentence must contain a subject and a verb. The writer can easily identify the subject in a sentence by asking the following questions:

1. Which part of the sentence is *performing* the action?
2. About which part of the sentence is something *being said?*
3. *Whom* is the sentence about?
4. *What* is the sentence about?

Examples: Incomplete Sentences
Arrested the suspect.
Searched the interior of the home.
Has a flat tire.

These words are missing an important factor—a subject. One must ask the following questions:

Who arrested the suspect?
Who searched the interior of the home?
What has a flat tire?

The subject represents the main topic or main idea of a sentence.

Examples: Complete Sentences
Officer Roberts arrested the suspect. (who)
Officer Johnson searched the interior of the home. (who)
The *patrol car* has a flat tire. (what)

Sometimes it is not easy to identify the subject of a sentence. When a word or group of words is written as a command, the subject is *you.*

Examples: (You) Write the arrest report!
                  (You) Don't move!
                  (You) Put your hands up!
                  (You) Wait!
                  (You) Stop!
                  (You) Run!

The subject in all six sentences is understood to be *you.*

Exercise 1

Directions: Underline the subject of each sentence.

Example: I enjoy writing reports.

1. Officer Ramirez apprehended the suspect.
2. During the trial, the defendant whispered something to his attorney.
3. At the scene of the crime, investigators found the murder weapon.
4. Fingerprints, which belonged to the suspect, appeared on the door.
5. Stop the car! (Remember the rule?)
6. Call the police! (Remember the rule?)
7. The magistrate signed the search warrant.
8. The evidence, which is in the lab, is marijuana.
9. The arrest report is clear and concise.
10. Gang members often use violence in order to intimidate their victims.

Score = (# correct × 10) = _____%

Exercise 2

Directions: Underline the subject of each sentence.

1. In the trunk of Palmer's car, Officer Sanchez found fifty pounds of cocaine.

2. Officer Talvin conducted a lawful search of the suspect's home.

3. Interpersonal communication skills are important for every officer.

4. While looking out of the window, Mrs. Smith saw the suspect running across the yard.

5. All of a sudden, the fire engulfed the entire room.

6. Thinking that an intruder was in her home, Terry called 911 right away.

7. A positive attitude contributes to a healthy lifestyle.

8. Because he worked hard and studied, Trainee Williams graduated with honors from the academy.

9. While they were in the gymnasium, the inmates started fighting.

10. Professional conduct, a daily requirement for every law enforcement and correctional officer, must never be compromised.

Score = (# correct × 10) = _____%

PART F

Capitalization

Writers of reports should be familiar with the following capitalization rules.

Rules to Remember

Rule 1. Capitalize the names of persons, cities, states, and streets.

    Examples: Chicago, Illinois, is experiencing a wave of violence.

                        Officer Taylor responded to 3210 Ocean Drive.

Rule 2. Capitalize organizations and buildings.

    Examples: The National Sheriffs' Association will be meeting next week.

                        The World Trade Center tragedies will not be forgotten.

Rule 3. Capitalize days, months, and holidays.

    Examples: Our class graduated from the training institute on Wednesday, June 1, 2002.

                        Dr. Martin Luther King Day addresses the importance of human rights.

Rule 4. Capitalize geographic locations.

> **Examples:**   Officer Coleman is from the North.
> The justice conference will be held in the South.

Note: Do not capitalize direction of travel.

> Incorrect: I was traveling South on I-95.
> Correct: I was traveling south on I-95.

Rule 5. Capitalize titles of professionals.

> **Examples:**   A luncheon will be held to honor Chief Jack Olson.
> I saw Judge William Gilbert on TV.

Rule 6. Capitalize the specific title of academic subjects.

> **Examples:**   The officer registered for Introduction to Criminology.
> On Monday, we take the Criminal Law 4118 final exam.

Rule 7. Capitalize brand names.

> **Examples:**   Corporal Hobbes retrieved a Smith & Wesson from the inmate's cell.
> Ms. Jones told me that her Sony television set had been stolen.

Rule 8. Capitalize the titles of films, books, and poems.

> **Examples:**   I highly recommend the *Report It in Writing* workbook.
> Every trainee should have a copy of the *Law Enforcement Handbook.*

Exercise 1

Directions: Underline the letter of the word(s) that should be capitalized.

Example: I spoke to major wertell about the homicide.

1. On saturday, I met with my study group to review for the test.

2. The national institute of justice reports a slight decline in the number of property crimes.

3. Sergeant Shapiro is moving to the west when he retires.

4. Officer Sheldon retrieved a smith & wesson from the suspect's pocket.

5. Lieutenant Johnson is taking public administration 6750 at the university.

6. Our class graduated on september 3, 1996.

7. A representative from the bureau of alcohol, tobacco, and firearms spoke with our class about procedural guidelines.

8. The officer arrested the defendant for stealing a pioneer stereo.

9. If you have any questions about report writing, ask professor Marilyn Meyers.

10. Does our class meet on thanksgiving?

Score = (# correct × 10) = _____%

Exercise 2

Directions: Underline the letter of the word(s) that should be capitalized.

Example: I interviewed <u>v</u>ictim <u>s</u>mith regarding the incident.

1. On tuesday, officer jackson and I questioned inmate jones about the incident.

2. The officer arrested the juvenile for stealing a rolex watch.

3. On december 14, 1997, lieutenant thurston was promoted.

4. Does our squad work on new year's day?

5. When the sergeant retires, he would like to move to the south.

6. The federal bureau of investigation reports a slight decline in overall crime rates.

7. I drove to 3140 ocean drive regarding a domestic disturbance.

8. sergeant sherman registered for introduction to criminology at the college.

9. This year's christmas party will be held at sergeant miller's house.

10. The suspect was wearing faded levi's blue jeans, a black and red miami heat cap, and a pair of reebok tennis shoes.

Score = (# correct × 10) = _____%

SECTION V

Active vs. Passive Voice, Subject and Verb Agreement, and Grammar

PART A

Active and Passive Voice

Rules to Remember

Unless your department requires otherwise, you should use the active voice as your primary style of writing.

The *active voice* style uses the subject of the sentence to perform the action.

The *passive voice* style uses the subject of the sentence to receive the action. Usually (not always), the passive structure contains the helping verb *was* and the preposition *by*.

Examples: The *inmate* filed a grievance. (active)

A grievance was filed by the *inmate*. (passive)

In the first example, the word *inmate performs* the action (filed).

In the second example, *inmate* performs the action on the subject *grievance*, which receives the action. *Inmate* follows the words *was* and *by*.

Examples: *Officer Kelly* submitted a memorandum for a raise. (active)

A memorandum for a raise was submitted by *Officer Kelly*. (passive)

Once again, in the first example, *Officer Kelly performs* the action (submitted).

In the second example, *Officer Kelly performs* the action on the subject *memorandum. Officer Kelly* follows the words *was* and *by*.

Active and Passive Voice

A verb is in the *active* voice when it expresses an *action performed by its subject*. A verb is in the *passive voice* when it expresses an *action performed upon its subject* or when the subject is the result of the action.

ACTIVE VOICE   The lightning struck the officer's vehicle.
PASSIVE VOICE The officer's vehicle was struck by lightning.

ACTIVE VOICE   The sergeant reviewed the report.
PASSIVE VOICE The report was reviewed by the sergeant.

As you can see, in the active examples, the subject performs the action. In the passive examples, the subject receives the action.

ACTIVE   Experienced officers write quality reports.
PASSIVE   Quality reports are written by experienced officers.

ACTIVE   The officer flashed the headlights.
PASSIVE   The headlights were flashed by the officer.

Exercise 1

Directions: On the blank provided, place an **A** if the sentence is written in the active voice. Place a **P** if the sentence is written in the passive voice.

Example: P The suspect was searched by Officer Daniels.

_____ 1. Officer Ramiro searched the interior of the car.

_____ 2. The evidence was gathered and secured by Officer Callahan.

_____ 3. Miranda warnings were read to the suspect by Officer Burton.

_____ 4. The drunk driver ran a stop sign.

_____ 5. The inmate tried to hide his weapon under the pillow.

_____ 6. The burglary was committed by the juvenile.

_____ 7. The car was stolen by me.

_____ 8. The weapon was retrieved by Officer Samuelson.

_____ 9. Officer Newton confiscated the drugs.

_____ 10. An emergency meeting was called by Lieutenant Greene.

Score = (# correct × 10) = _____%

Exercise 2

Directions: On the blank provided, place an **A** if the sentence is written in the active voice. Place a **P** if the sentence is written in the passive voice.

Example: P The report was read by the sergeant.

_____ 1. Officer Reed searched the cell.

_____ 2. The cell was searched by Officer Reed.

_____ 3. The officer wrote the report.

_____ 4. The report was written by the officer.

_____ 5. Information about the incident was provided by the inmate.

_____ 6. The inmate provided information about the incident.

_____ 7. The subject was transported to the station.

_____ 8. I transported the subject to the station.

_____ 9. Fire Rescue #27 was called to the scene.

_____ 10. I called Fire Rescue #27 to the scene.

Score = (# correct × 10) = _____%

Exercise 3

Directions: On the blank provided, place an **A** if the sentence is written in the active voice. Place a **P** if the sentence is written in the passive voice.

_____ 1. The subject was taken to Jackson Crisis by me.

_____ 2. Heavy rains flooded the streets.

_____ 3. Police directs traffic.

_____ 4. The offender was arrested by my partner.

_____ 5. Rocks and bottles were thrown by the crowd.

_____ 6. Victim Jones was stabbed in the chest by Suspect Smith.

_____ 7. Vehicle #2 struck the light pole.

_____ 8. In the living room, the homicide victim was found.

_____ 9. I searched the prisoner.

_____ 10. In the suspect's right front pants pocket, a small plastic bag containing suspected cocaine was found by me.

Score = (# correct × 10) = _____%

Exercise 4

Directions: Each sentence is written in the passive voice. Rewrite each sentence using the active voice.

Example: A decision was reached by the selection committee. (passive)

The selection committee reached a decision. (active)

1. The murder weapon was found by the investigator.

_____

2. A startling sound was heard by Mrs. Meyers.

_____

3. A knife was brought to school by the juvenile.

_____

4. The psychological exam was failed by the candidate.

_____

5. The suspect was arrested by Officer Reyes.

_____

6. The child was abducted by the stranger.

_____

7. The speech was given by Captain King.

   _____

8. The new recruits were welcomed by Chief Fitzgerald.

   _____

9. Identification was left by the robber.

   _____

10. The suspect was identified by the witness.

   _____

Score = (# correct × 10) = _____%

Exercise 5

Directions: Each sentence is written in the passive voice. Rewrite each sentence using the active voice.

Example: The promotional exam was passed by the officer. (passive)
The officer passed the promotional exam. (active)

1. The inmate was detained by Officer Nelson.

   _____

2. The handbook was given to the inmate by me.

   _____

3. The book was studied by the class.

   _____

4. The scene was secured by Officer Ramos.

   _____

5. The inmate was transported by me.

   _____

6. The witness was questioned by Officer Johnson.

   _____

7. A chain-link fence was hit by the vehicle.

   _____

8. Evidence was gathered by the sergeants.

   _____

9. The officer was kicked in the abdomen by the inmate.

   _____

10. The witnesses were interviewed by the detectives.

   _____

Score = (# correct × 10) = _____%

PART B

Subject and Verb Agreement

As a child, I enjoyed going to the park and playing on the seesaw. As a mom, I enjoy going to the park and playing on the seesaw with our sons. In order for the seesaw to balance, two individuals need to have a comparable weight. Clearly, if one person's weight far exceeds the other's, the seesaw will not balance.

The same principle can be applied to writing. If the words are not in harmony, the sentence will not be balanced. More specifically, if the subject and verb do not agree in form, the sentence will be incorrect, and the writer's work will look sloppy. Your departments do not want your written work to look sloppy; they want it to look professional.

When your work looks professional, you look professional. In Section IV, you studied the way a writer can identify the subject in a sentence (by asking *who* performed the action or *what* is the sentence about).

Once you have identified the subject of a sentence, you will have an easier time identifying the appropriate verb.

Rule to Remember

A *singular subject* must have a *singular verb*.

S   V

Example: The <u>officer</u> <u>wants</u> to visit Jamaica.

officer (singular subject) = wants (singular verb)

Rule to Remember

A *plural subject* is followed by a *plural verb*.

S   V

Example: The <u>officers</u> <u>want</u> to visit Jamaica.

officers (plural subject) = want (plural verb)

Exercise 1

Singular	Plural
badge	badges
uniform	uniforms
sergeant	sergeants
officer	officers
report	reports

Directions: Using the above word list, select the appropriate word for each sentence. (*Hint:* Look carefully at the verb.)

1. The _____ <u>has searched</u> the interior of the suspect's car.

2. The _____ <u>have searched</u> the interior of the suspect's car.

3. The _____ <u>reads</u> all of the arrest reports.

4. The _____ <u>read</u> all of the arrest reports.

5. The _____ <u>are</u> well written.

6. The _____ <u>is</u> well written.

7. The _____ <u>needs</u> to be shined.

8. The _____ <u>need</u> to be shined.

9. The _____ <u>looks</u> very impressive.

10. The _____ <u>looks</u> very impressive.

Score = (# correct × 10) = _____%

Exercise 2

SINGULAR	PLURAL
gun	guns
suspect	suspects
chief	chiefs
inmate	inmate
juvenile	juveniles

Directions: Using the word list above, select the appropriate word for each sentence.

1. The _____ was arrested for aggravated battery.

2. The _____ were arrested for armed robbery.

3. The _____ has a wooden hand grip.

4. The _____ have wooden hand grips.

5. The _____ is speaking to the captain.

6. The _____ are reviewing the community-policing project.

7. The _____ has been released on parole.

8. The _____ have been released on parole.

9. The _____ is attending classes at boot camp.

10. The _____ are attending classes at boot camp.

Score = (# correct × 10) = _____%

PART C

Pronoun Agreement

You should remember to consider the role of pronouns in balancing subjects and verbs.

Rule to Remember

The following **pronouns,** which are often used as subjects, are *always singular:*

SINGULAR PRONOUNS

each
either
every
neither
one

Incorrect:	1a. Each of the officers have mastered writing skills.
Correct:	1b. *Each* of the officers *has* mastered writing skills.
Incorrect:	2a. Neither of the attorneys have filed a motion.
Correct:	2b. *Neither* of the attorneys *has* filed a motion.
Incorrect:	3a. Every inmate in Wing B have a violent temper.
Correct:	3b. *Every* inmate in Wing B *has* a violent temper.
Incorrect:	4a. One of the inmates are responsible for the fire.
Correct:	4b. *One* of the inmates *is* responsible for the fire.
Incorrect:	5a. Either of the sergeants are capable of handling the job.
Correct:	5b. *Either* of the sergeants *is* capable of handling the job.

Remember the seesaw: Both sides must balance.
Remember the sentence: The subject and verb must balance.
All of the *a* responses are unbalanced.

Rule to Remember

The following pronouns, which are often used as subjects, *are plural*:

PLURAL PRONOUNS

many
few
both
neither
several

Incorrect: 1a. Many of the inmates needs counseling.
Correct: 1b. *Many* of the inmates *need* counseling.

Incorrect: 2a. Few of the inmates is trustworthy.
Correct: 2b. *Few* of the inmates *are* trustworthy.

Incorrect: 3a. Both of the inmates has violent tempers.
Correct: 3b. *Both* of the inmates *have* violent tempers.

Incorrect: 4a. Several of the inmates is released every day.
Correct: 4b. *Several* of the inmates *are* released every day.

You should concentrate on learning the correct usage. If necessary, memorize the pronouns and how they are used so that you will be able to use them appropriately in your written work.

Rule to Remember

Professional writers must *always* remember that there are *exceptions* to rules. Some pronouns can be singular or plural, depending upon how they are used in a sentence.

When using pronouns in your written work, consider the following exceptions:

PRONOUN EXCEPTIONS

some
none
most
all

Incorrect: 1a. Some of the inmates is able to successfully rehabilitate.
Correct: 1b. *Some* of the inmates *are* able to successfully rehabilitate.

In sentence 1b, <u>some</u> refers to the plural *inmates;* therefore, the plural verb *are* is correct.

Incorrect: 2a. Some of the cocaine were confiscated.
Correct: 2b. *Some* of the cocaine *was confiscated.*

In sentence 2b, <u>some</u> refers to singular *cocaine;* therefore, the verb *was confiscated* is singular.

Incorrect: 3a. None of the amphetamines was found.
Correct: 3b. *None* of the amphetamines *were found.*

In sentence 3b, <u>none</u> refers to the plural *amphetamines;* therefore, the verb *were found* is plural.

Incorrect: 4a. None of the material were reviewed.
Correct: 4b. *None* of the material *was reviewed.*

In sentence 4b, <u>none</u> refers to the singular *material;* therefore, the verb *was reviewed* is singular.

Incorrect: 5a. Most of the guns was smuggled into this
               country.
Correct: 5b. *Most* of the guns *were smuggled* into this
               country.

In sentence 5b, <u>most</u> refers to the plural *guns;* therefore, the verb *were smuggled* is plural.

Incorrect: 6a. Most of the evidence were sent to the lab.
Correct: 6b. *Most* of the evidence *was sent* to the lab.

In sentence 6b, <u>most</u> refers to the singular *evidence;* therefore, the verb *was sent* is singular.

Incorrect: 7a. All of the officers has written their reports.
Correct: 7b. *All* of the officers *have written* their reports.

In sentence 7a, <u>all</u> refers to the plural *officers;* therefore, the verb *have written* is plural.

Incorrect: 8a. All of the work have been approved.
Correct: 8b. *All* of the work *has been approved.*

In sentence 8b, <u>all</u> refers to the singular work; therefore, the verb *has been approved* is singular.

Exercise 1

Directions: On the blank provided, identify the correct form of the verb in parentheses.

_____ 1. Neither of the inmates (have, has) been released.

_____ 2. Each of the trainees (call, calls) home at noon.

_____ 3. One of the inmates (is, are) late for the hearing.

_____ 4. Every defendant (has, have) constitutional rights.

_____ 5. Several juveniles (has, have) been arrested.

_____ 6. Either of the officers (is, are) capable of handling the job.

_____ 7. Each of the officers (care, cares) about his or her community.

_____ 8. Every inmate (looks, look) forward to going home.

_____ 9. Neither of the officers (has, have) called in sick.

_____ 10. Several of the prisoners (have, has) been released on parole.

Score = (# correct × 10) = _____%

Exercise 2

Directions: On the blank provided, identify the correct form of the verb in parentheses.

_____ 1. Neither of the suspects (have, has) been arrested.

_____ 2. Either of the sergeants (is, are) going to the meeting.

_____ 3. Both of the trainees (is, are) doing well in class.

_____ 4. Each of the reports (have, has) been approved.

_____ 5. Neither of the sergeants (has, have) written a disciplinary report.

_____ 6. Each of the lieutenants (is, are) being promoted today.

_____ 7. All of the captains (is, are) retiring in December.

_____ 8. Neither of the juveniles (was, were) at the crime scene.

_____ 9. Both of the officers (is, are) motivated to succeed.

_____ 10. Each of the trainees (is, are) doing well at the academy.

Score = (# correct × 10) = _____%

Exercise 3

Directions: On the blank provided, identify the correct form of the verb in parentheses.

_____ 1. Some of the inmates (is, are) able to reintegrate into free society.

_____ 2. Some of the evidence (has, have) been confiscated and brought to the lab.

_____ 3. None of the officers (is, are) going on vacation.

_____ 4. None of the cells (has, have) been searched.

_____ 5. Most of the weapons (belong, belongs) to the Mafia.

_____ 6. Most of the juveniles (have, has) been released.

_____ 7. All of the reports (are, is) well written.

_____ 8. All of the material (is, are) documented.

_____ 9. Some of the sergeants (have, has) read the reports.

_____ 10. All of the trainees (have, has) passed the state exam.

Score = (# correct × 10) = _____%

Exercise 4

Directions: On the blank provided, identify the correct form of the verb in parentheses.

_____ 1. Neither of the suspects (has, have) been arrested.

_____ 2. Either of the sergeants (is, are) going to the meeting.

_____ 3. Several of the juveniles (has, have) been approved.

_____ 4. Each of the reports (has, have) been approved.

_____ 5. Every officer (looks, look) forward to a vacation.

_____ 6. Each of the lieutenants (is, are) being promoted today.

_____ 7. All of the captains (is, are) retiring in December.

_____ 8. Both of the officers (is, are) motivated to succeed.

_____ 9. Neither of the juveniles (was, were) at the crime scene.

_____ 10. Each of the trainees (is, are) doing well in class.

Score = (# correct × 10) = _____%

SECTION VI

Spelling

Rule to Remember

Spelling is a weakness for many writers. Quality report writers cannot afford to make spelling mistakes. Why? Spelling mistakes damage the writer's professionalism. Remember that your department is not paying you to make errors. Mistakes are costly; they can result in departmental liability. There are spelling rules that are easy to remember. Review these eighteen easy spelling rules. Share them with your friends and colleagues who are trying to improve their spelling.

Rule 1. *i* comes before *e.*

    Examples: p**ie**ce, bel**ie**ve, ch**ie**f

Exceptions to the *i* before *e* spelling rule

counterf**ei**t	h**ei**ght	s**ei**ze	w**ei**ght
either	h**ei**nous	s**ei**zure	w**ei**rd
for**ei**gner	l**ei**sure	sover**ei**gn	
forf**ei**t	n**ei**ther	th**ei**r	

Rule 2. *e* comes before *i* after *c.*

    Examples: rec**ei**ve,   c**ei**ling,   rec**ei**pt

Rule 3. *e* comes before *i* that has a long *a sound.*

    Examples: **ei**ght,   w**ei**ght,   n**ei**ghbor

Rule 4. Write the *prefix* + the *word.*

    Examples: *re* + commend = recommend
                        dis + appear   = disappear
                        il + legal   = illegal

193

Rule 5. Write the **word** + the **suffix.**

Examples:	sincere	+ **ly**	= sincerely
	depart	+ **ment**	= department
	agree	+ **able**	= agreeable

Rule 6. To form the plural, change the **y** to **i** when a consonant comes before the **y.**

Examples:	bod**y**	= bod**i**es
	lad**y**	= lad**i**es
	bab**y**	= bab**i**es

Rule 7. To form the plural, change the **f** to **v.**

Examples:	wi**f**e	= wi**v**es
	kni**f**e	= kni**v**es
	li**f**e	= li**v**es

Rule 8. To form the plural, change vowels **a** or **o** to **e.**

Examples:	m**a**n	= m**e**n
	wom**a**n	= wom**e**n
	t**oo**th	= t**ee**th

Rule 9. When adding a suffix that begins with a vowel, drop the silent **e.**

Examples:	advis**e**	= advis**ing**
	argu**e**	= argu**ing**
	judg**e**	= judg**ing**

Rule 10. Add **able** to words that **can** stand alone.

Examples:	avail	+ **able**	= avail**able**
	depend	+ **able**	= depend**able**
	knowledge	+ **able**	= knowledge**able**

Rule 11. Add **ary** to words that **cannot** stand alone.

Examples:	auxili	+ **ary**	= auxili**ary**
	burgl	+ **ary**	= burgl**ary**
	milit	+ **ary**	= milit**ary**

Rule 12. Add **ible** to words that **cannot** stand alone.

Examples:	admiss	+ **ible**	= admiss**ible**
	elig	+ **ible**	= elig**ible**
	forc	+ **ible**	= forc**ible**

Rule 13. Add *ory* to words that *can* stand alone.

	Examples:				
	audit	+	*ory*	=	audit*ory*
	direct	+	*ory*	=	direct*ory*
	invent	+	*ory*	=	invent*ory*

Rule 14. Add *ous* to words that *can* stand alone.

	Examples:				
	courage	+	*ous*	=	courage*ous*
	humor	+	*ous*	=	humor*ous*
	rigor	+	*ous*	=	rigor*ous*

Rule 15. Double the final consonant when:

1. The last letter is a single consonant.
2. A single vowel comes before the last consonant.
3. The accent is on the last syllable.

	Examples:		
	commit	=	commi***tt***ed
	occur	=	occu***rr***ed
	patrol	=	patro***ll***ed

Rule 16. Double the final consonant in a one-syllable word when a single vowel comes before the final consonant.

	Examples:		
	run	=	ru***nn***ing
	sit	=	si***tt***ing
	stop	=	sto***pp***ing

Rule 17. To form the past tense, change *y* to *i* and then add a *d.*

	Examples:		
	lay	=	la***id***
	pay	=	pa***id***
	say	=	sa***id***

Rule 18. Use *ian* for words relating to a title or occupation.

	Examples:	
	electric*ian,* physic*ian,* technic*ian*	

Note: Remember there are exceptions to the rules. When in doubt, consult a dictionary.

Ten Easy Ways to Improve Your Spelling

Good Point　1.　Refer to the list of commonly misspelled words in the workbook.

Good Point　2.　Refer to a dictionary.

Good Point　3.　Use an electronic spelling device.

Good Point　4.　Learn one new spelling rule each week.

Good Point　5.　Practice spelling words commonly used in the profession.

Good Point　6.　Substitute an easy word for a difficult word. (I spell *concurrence* **a-g-r-e-e.**)

Good Point　7.　Look for hints in the word. (The word *tomorrow* is the spelling of three words: tom/or/row.)

Good Point　8.　Help your colleagues improve their spelling by posting a weekly list of misspelled words that appeared on reports or memos. (That will get their attention!)

Good Point　9.　Spell words that are giving you difficulty into a tape recorder. Each evening, listen actively to the tape.

Good Point 10.　Maintain a positive attitude and practice, practice, practice!

Good Point 11.　Write words that you often misspell on flash cards. Study them when you have time. Have your friends quiz you with the cards.

Good Point 12.　Read, read, read! The more you read, the more you'll be exposed to new words and how they are spelled correctly.

Smart Spelling Sentences

Use Hints: Write the words that you find challenging in sentences. Underline the part of the word that gives you difficulty.

Examples:　The lieutenant uses a pen in lieu of a pencil.
The complainant complained about ants in the court.
Barbi's barbiturates are saturated.
Hand Chief Ker a handkerchief.
He schemed to leave school early.
Tomorrow Tom will review the reports.
The trusty at the jail trusts you.
A pro proceeds to succeed.
The kid took a nap.
The movie Sepa is rated G.

Exercise 1

Directions: Using five spelling words, create your own smart spelling sentences.

1. _____

2. _____

3. _____

4. _____

5. _____

Exercise 2

Directions: On the blank provided before the number, write the word that is spelled correctly.

_____ 1. I (believe, beleive) the victim's testimony.

_____ 2. The (cheif, chief) will speak at the luncheon.

_____ 3. The suspect dropped a (piece, peice) of clothing at the scene.

_____ 4. I (received, recieved) a call from the sergeant.

_____ 5. The officer found a (reciept, receipt) in the inmate's cell.

_____ 6. The officer's (cieling, ceiling) caved in during the storm.

_____ 7. Officer Kelly arrested (eight, ieght) juveniles for motor vehicle theft.

_____ 8. The inmate's (wieght, weight) is approximately 200 pounds.

_____ 9. The (nieghbor, neighbor) called the police.

_____ 10. I (recommend, reccomend) Officer Smith for the position.

Score = (# correct × 10) _____%

Exercise 3

Directions: On the blank provided before the number, write the word that is spelled correctly.

_____ 1. The investigator found the (bodies, bodys).

_____ 2. The rapist victimized elderly (ladys, ladies).

_____ 3. The officers seized two (knifes, knives) from the inmate's cell.

_____ 4. The witness saw the inmate (runing, running) down the street.

_____ 5. The officers are (planing, planning) a surprise party for Sergeant Wilson.

_____ 6. Officer Brown (patrolled, patroled) the area at 0900 hours.

_____ 7. The defendant said he (committed, commited) the murder.

_____ 8. The incident (occured, occurred) at 2300 hours.

_____ 9. I (sincerely, sincerly) appreciate your service to the community.

_____ 10. There should be zero tolerance for (ilegal, illegal) conduct.

Score = (# correct × 10) = _____%

Exercise 4

Directions: On the blank provided before the number, write the word that is spelled correctly.

_____ 1. The inmate has been (incarcerated, incarserated) for four months.

_____ 2. The woman (identifyed, identified) the suspect in the lineup.

_____ 3. The juvenile's parents (separated, seperated) when he was a baby.

_____ 4. I (heard, heared) the elderly woman scream for help.

_____ 5. I (commanded, commandded) the suspect to drop his gun; he refused.

_____ 6. The officer was (exhausted, exausted) after the chase.

_____ 7. The suspect (argued, argude) with me for fifteen minutes.

_____ 8. Inmate Smith said that Jones (coerced, coersed) him to start the fight.

_____ 9. The officer was (disapointed, disappointed) about the outcome of the case.

_____ 10. The fugitive (assaultted, assaulted) the child.

Score = (# correct × 10) = _____%

Exercise 5

Directions: On the blank provided before the number, write the word that is spelled correctly.

_____ 1. The suspect said he (abductted, abducted) the child.

_____ 2. The officer's use of force is (justifyed, justified) by probable cause.

_____ 3. I (patroled, patrolled) the area where the rape took place.

_____ 4. The inmate was (parolled, paroled) yesterday morning.

_____ 5. The juvenile (denyed, denied) participating in the robbery.

_____ 6. The house is (equiped, equipped) with an effective alarm system.

_____ 7. The woman (changed, changged) her testimony during the trial.

_____ 8. The inmate (managed, mannaged) to escape from prison.

_____ 9. During dinner, a fight (developed, developped) among the inmates.

_____ 10. The officer (fulfilled, fullfilled) her duties in a professional manner.

Score = (# correct × 10) = _____%

Exercise 6

Directions: On the blank provided before the number, write the word that is spelled correctly.

_____ 1. The witness said, "The guy (actted, acted) like he was on drugs."

_____ 2. I (believed, beleived) what the witness told me.

_____ 3. The officer (comforted, comfroted) the frightened child.

_____ 4. The store owner said the suspect (committed, commitcd) the robbery.

_____ 5. The suspect (deserted, desertted) the stolen car near the highway.

_____ 6. The burglar (enterred, entered) the home through an open window.

_____ 7. The inmate is (interested, intrested) in the work release program.

_____ 8. The officer (pursued, persued) the suspect for twenty minutes.

_____ 9. The witness (testifyed, testified) at the trial.

_____ 10. The expert witness was (paid, payed) $100 for her time.

Score = (# correct × 10) _____%

Exercise 7

Directions: On the blank provided, write the appropriate ending from the following options.

> *tion*
> *cian*
> *sion*
> *cion*
> *xion*

_____   1. The witness gave me a descrip _____ of the suspect.

_____   2. I saw a man with a tan comple _____ leave the bank.

_____   3. Communica _____ skills are important for every officer.

_____   4. The techni _____ filed a complaint against her boss.

_____   5. Officer Houston suffered a concus _____ during the armed robbery.

_____   6. Mr. Murphy sued Ms. Burton for defama _____ of character.

_____   7. Coer _____ is considered an inappropriate form of conduct.

_____   8. The graduation ceremony at the academy is a memorable occa _____ .

_____   9. Mr. Carter showed signs of public intoxica _____ .

_____ 10. The criminal justice profes _____ offers many challenging opportunities.

Score = (# correct × 10) = _____%

Exercise 8

Directions: On the blank provided, write the appropriate ending from the following options.

ence
ance
ience

_____ 1. The courts must strike a bal _____between the individual's rights and the state's interest.

_____ 2. I was dispatched to 9763 Park Lane regarding a domestic disturb _____ .

_____ 3. Confid _____ is an important attribute for criminal justice professionals.

_____ 4. We set up a perimeter around the circumfer _____ of the prison.

_____ 5. I arrested the defendant because she was driving under the influ _____ of alcohol.

_____ 6. Viol _____ is an unfortunate reality in every state.

_____ 7. During adolesc _____, some teenagers experiment with narcotics.

_____ 8. Mr. Jasper violated the newly implemented ordin _____ .

_____ 9. I responded to a robbery call at the conven _____ store.

_____ 10. Officers should conduct themselves in accord with department policy and procedures.

Score = (# correct × 10) = _____%

Exercise 9

Directions: On the blank provided, write the appropriate past tense form of the verb in parentheses.

Remember the *y* to *i* rule.

1. I (try) _____ to control the members of the crowd, but they continued to throw bottles.

2. The officer's stop was (justify) _____ by probable cause.

3. The witness (say) _____ the suspect drove away in a gray van.

4. The officer (lay) _____ the report on the sergeant's desk.

5. According to the officer's report, Smith (bury) _____ the body in the yard.

6. The juvenile (envy) _____ his older brother, who owns a Corvette.

7. The inmate (qualify) _____ for the work release program.

8. Officer McPherson (simplify) _____ the report narrative.

9. The detectives were (mystify) _____ by the lack of evidence at the crime scene.

10. Because he (falsify) _____ a government document, the executive was arrested.

Score = (# correct × 10) = _____%

Exercise 10

Directions: On the blank provided, write the appropriate ending from the following options.

ize
ise
ice
yze

_____ 1. The captain will anal _____ the community policing project.

_____ 2. I adv _____ you to consult with an attorney.

_____ 3. Here is free adv _____: Control your emotions before your emotions control you.

_____ 4. The victim was paral _____d after the bullet penetrated his spine.

_____ 5. Familiar _____ yourself with the rules and policies of your department.

_____ 6. The paramedic steril _____d the needle before she injected it into the victim's arm.

_____ 7. You should not internal _____ your stress; instead, you should find ways to manage it.

_____ 8. Many law enforcement representatives regard exerc _____ as a positive way to relieve tension.

_____ 9. I tried tw _____ to reach the chief, but he is out of town.

_____ 10. We coordinated a surpr _____ party for the major, who is retiring next week.

Score = (# correct × 10) = _____%

Exercise 11

Directions: Write ten words that you frequently misspell.

1. _____
2. _____
3. _____
4. _____
5. _____
6. _____
7. _____
8. _____
9. _____
10. _____

Exercise 12

Directions: Your instructor will ask you to correctly spell ten words from the spelling list beginning on the next page.

1. _____
2. _____
3. _____
4. _____
5. _____
6. _____
7. _____
8. _____
9. _____
10. _____

SPELLING LIST

A

action
administrative
affective
appendix
argument
assault
attitude
authoritative
authorize
automatic
auxiliary

B

bachelor
bail
balance
ballistics
barbiturate
barracks
barrage
barrel
barricade
basic
battery
beginning
behavior
believe
belligerent
beneficiary
benefit
bicycle
boisterous
bookkeeper
border
boundary
boycott
brakes
breath
bruise
brunette
bullet
bulletin
bureau
burglary
burst
business
buttocks

C

cafeteria
calculate
calendar
caliber
candidate
capable
capital
captain
carburetor
cardiac
carnal
cartridge
catastrophe
catholic
caution
ceiling
cellophane
celluloid
cemetery
censor
ceremony
certain
certificate
challenge
champion
changeable
chaos
character
chased
chemical
chief
chiropractor
chisel
chloroform
choose
chose
chosen
chrome
cigarette
circular
circumference
circumstantial
citation
classification
clearance
clemency
clerical

client
clothes
coach
coagulate
coax
cocaine
coercion
collar
collusion
colonel
column
coma
comfortable
commanded
commerce
commission
committed
committee
communicate
companion
compass
compelled
competent
complainant
complexion
comprehensible
concede
concur
concussion
condemn
confidence
confinement
confiscate
confrontation
conjecture
conscious
consecutive
contempt
continued
continuously
contraband
copulation
coronary
corporal
corpse
correspond
corroborate
corroded

council
counselor
counterfeit
courageous
courteous
credible
creditable
criminal
critical
cruelty
custody
custom
cylinder

D

daring
debt
deceased
deceive
decency
deception
decipher
decisive
decontaminate
decrease
deduction
defamation
defendant
defense
deferred
defiant
deficiency
definite
definitely
defraud
delayed
delete
delicate
delinquent
delirious
delusion
denial
denied
density
dependent
depression
descent
description
desert

designate
desperate
destitute
destroyed
detail
detainer
detective
detention
develop
deviate
diabetes
diagnosis
diagonal
dialect
diamond
difference
different
difficult
dilapidated
dilemma
disagree
disagreeable
disappear
disappoint
disciplinary
discipline
discontinued
discrepancy
disease
disguise
disheveled
disinfectant
disintegrate
disobedient
disperse
disposed
disqualification
distinguish
distress
disturbance
divide
divulge
docket
doctor
document
drill
drills
drizzle
drunkenness

duplex
during
dutiful
dying

E

earnest
easily
eccentric
echo
edible
education
effect
effective
efficient
ejaculated
ejected
elaborate
elbow
electricity
elementary
elevated
eligible
eliminate
eloquent
embalm
embedded
embraced
emergency
emphasis
employee
enclosure
encounter
endorsement
endured
enemy
enforcement
engaged
engraving
enormous
entailed
entered
enthusiasm
envelop
environment
episode
equilibrium
equipment
equipped

erase
erotic
erroneous
error
escrow
especially
essential
establish
estimation
ether
ethical
evacuation
evaporate
evasive
evidence
exaggerate
examined
excellent
excess
excitement
excuse
execute
exemption
exercise
exhausted
exhibitionist
existence
exonerate
expectancy
expedite
experience
experiment
explanation
exterior
extinguish
extravagant
extremely

F
facility
faculty
falsified
familiarize
fascinate
fasten
fatality
faulty
feasible
features

feign
felony
feminine
feverish
field
fiend
fiery
fifteen
financial
flare
flexible
flippant
fluid
forehead
foreign
foreman
forfeit
formally
fornication
forty
fraction
fraudulent
freight
frequency
friend
fugitive
fulfill
fumigate
furlough
furniture

G
garble
gasoline
gauge
genuine
glaring
gnaw
government
grammar
grievance
guarantee
guard
guide

H
habitual
hallucination
handkerchief

happiness
health
hearing
heavy
height
heroin
heroism
holiday
homicide
homosexual
horrible
humane
humorous
hurried
hydraulic
hydrogen
hygiene
hysterical

I
identical
identified
identify
ignition
ignorant
illinois
illiterate
illusion
imitate
immaterial
immature
immediately
imminent
immoral
impersonate
impertinent
implement
implicate
implied
impossible
incapacitated
incarceration
incest
incident
incoherent
incompatible
incompetence
inconvenience

independent
index
indication
indict
indispensable
individual
indulgence
infection
inferior
infinite
influence
informant
ingenious
inhale
inherit
initiate
innocence
inquired
insanity
insert
insinuate
insisted
inspector
instantaneous
institution
instrument
insufficient
integrate
intelligence
intelligible
intention
intercept
interest
interior
interpret
interrogate
intersect
intersection
interval
intervene
interview
intestinal
intimate
intoxication
intuition
investigation
invincible
irrational
irrelevant
irritable

J
jewelry
judgment
judicial
jurisdiction
justified

K
kerosene
kidnap
knowledge

L
lab
label
laboratory
laborer
lacerate
ladder
language
larynx
laundry
law
lax
league
lease
legitimate
leisure
length
lesbian
liability
liable
libel
library
license
licentious
lieutenant
lightning
liquid
list
listen
literature
livelihood
logical
longitude
loose
lose
lucid
luxury
lying

M
machine
magistrate
magnetic
maintenance
malfeasance
manageable
manager
manicurist
manual
manufacturer
margin
marijuana
marital
marriage
masquerade
mathematics
mayor
measure
medicine
mentality
merited
mileage
military
miniature
minimum
minor
minute
mirror
miscellaneous
modern
modify
momentum
monotonous
morale
morbid
morphine
motivated
motive
mucous
muffler
multiple
murmur
muscle
mustache
mutiny

N
narcotic
necessary

negligence
negligible
negotiable
neighbor
neither
nephew
nicotine
noticeable

O

obedient
obsessive
obstruction
occasion
occurred
offense
officer
omitted
opaque
operate
opponent
opposite
optimistic
origin
orphan
orthodox
oxygen

P

paid
pale
palm
pamphlet
panel
paraffin
parallel
paralyzed
paraphernalia
parole
partition
pastime
patient
patrol
patrolled
peaceably
penalty
penitentiary
people
perforate
perform

perjury
perpetrate
perseverance
personal
personnel
perspire
persuade
phony
pierce
platoon
plausible
plea
plexiglas
poison
positive
positively
possession
practice
precarious
preceding
precious
prejudice
premise
presume
preventive
principal
principle
prisoner
privilege
procedure
proceed
profanity
profession
projectile
prominent
promiscuous
proprietor
prosecutor
prostration
proxy
psychiatrist
psychology
puncture
pursue
pyromaniac

Q

quarrel
quiet
quite

R

ransom
receipt
receive
recommend
reference
regret
regular
regulations
rehabilitate
reinforce
relationship
relevant
relieve
remedy
remnant
removable
repetition
repossess
reprimand
respiration
restaurant
restitution
rhythm

S

sabotage
sacrifice
sanitation
saturate
scene
scheme
scissors
screech
secrecy
secretary
sedation
seducing
seized
sensible
sensitive
separate
separated
september
sergeant
serial
several
sheriff
shriek
similar

siphon
siren
situated
skeptical
slander
slippery
smoldering
smooth
social
society
solemn
solicit
solution
specimen
spectator
spelling
spontaneous
squeal
stadium
stampede
stationary
stationery
statutory
stereotype
sterilize
stethoscope
straight
strength
stretch
stripped
structure
substantial
substitute
subtle
succeed
successful
suction
suggestive
suicide
sulfur
superintendent
superior
superstition
surgeon
surreptitious
suspicion
sweating
symptom

syringe
system

T
tactics
tangible
tattoo
technical
telegraph
tendency
tension
terminology
testicle
testified
thorough
tobacco
tongue
tonsil
tragedy
transient
transparent
trespass
trusty
tunnel
twelfth

U
ultimate
unkempt
using

V
vaccinate
vacuum
vague
variety
vaseline
vault
vegetable
vehicle
velocity
ventilate
verify
vertical
veteran
vicious
vigilance
violate

violent
visual

W
waist
warrant
weather
weight
weird
welfare
whiskey
whistle
wrecked
writing

Y
yesterday
yield

SECTION VII

Punctuation

Writers of reports should be familiar with marks of punctuation. Specifically, you should be comfortable using the comma, semi-colon, colon, quotation marks, and apostrophe.

PART A

The Comma

Rules to Remember

Rule 1. Use a comma to separate two complete sentences that are joined by a coordinating conjunction (*and, but, or, nor, for, yet*).

> **Examples:** Smith told me he heard a woman screaming, *and* he dialed 911.
> Inmate Jones was in the cafeteria, *but* he said he did not see who started the fight.

Rule 2. Use a comma after an introductory clause.

> **Examples:** When Officer Moss searched the *car*, she found a knife on the front seat.
> Because he consistently *studied*, Trainee Dennis graduated from the academy.

Rule 3. Use a comma to separate items in a series. A series consists of three or more items.

> **Examples:** Detective Wilson had fish, salad, and fruit for lunch.
> Sergeant Montgomery found knives, pins, and tacks underneath the inmate's mattress.

Rule 4. Use a comma to separate nonrestrictive (unimportant) phrases in a sentence. A phrase is a group of words that does not make a complete statement; it is considered nonrestrictive when no pertinent information is lost without it.

> **Examples:** Fingerprints, which officers found on the wall, belonged to the suspect.
> The car, which has black-tinted windows, was used in last night's robbery.

215

Rule 5. Use a comma between two or more adjectives that are not joined by *and* when they precede the noun.

Examples: Captain Gilbert is an intelligent, professional administrator.

Inmate Murphy is a cooperative, motivated trusty.

Rule 6. Use a comma to introduce a quote.

Examples: The witness told me, "The guy took a pipe and smashed the window of the Lexus."

The inmate said, "Get the hell outta here!"

Rule 7. Use a comma when writing dates.

Examples: On January 1, 2005, Inmate Jones was released on parole.

Our class will graduate on December 13, 2010.

Rule 8. Use a comma after the salutation of an informal letter.

Examples: Dear Aunt Margaret,

Dear Uncle Joe,

PART B

The Comma Splice

Rules to Remember

A comma splice is considered an incorrect mark of punctuation. It often occurs when a report writer uses a comma to join two complete sentences.

> **Example:** Officer McNeil arrested the suspect, he read him the Miranda warnings.
> The comma splice can be corrected in several ways.

Rule 1. The comma splice can be corrected by inserting a coordinating conjunction (*and, but, or, nor, for, yet, so*) after the comma.

> **Example:** Officer McNeil arrested the suspect, and he read him the Miranda warnings.

Rule 2. The comma splice can be corrected by inserting a *semicolon*.

> **Example:** Officer McNeil arrested the suspect; he read him the Miranda warnings.

Rule 3. The comma splice can be corrected by inserting *a period and making two complete statements*.

> **Example:** Officer McNeil arrested the suspect. He read him the Miranda warnings.

Rule 4. The comma splice can be corrected by writing one sentence as a *dependent clause*, which is a group of words with a subject and verb but doesn't make a complete sentence.

> **Example:** *After Officer McNeil arrested the suspect*, he read him the Miranda warnings.

PART C

The Semicolon

Rules to Remember

Rule 1. Use a semicolon to join two complete sentences that are not joined by a coordinating conjunction.

> **Examples:** The juveniles started fighting; the officer called for backup.
> The trainees studied for the test; they all passed.

Rule 2. Use a semicolon to join two complete sentences that are joined by a conjunctive adverb.
> The following words are conjunctive adverbs:

> **however**
> **therefore**
> **then**
> **for example**

> **Examples:** The defendant pleaded insanity; however, he was sentenced to twenty years in prison.
> Trainee Suarez exercises everyday; therefore, she usually feels relaxed and healthy.

Rule 3. Use a semicolon to separate clauses that already have commas.

> **Examples:** Crime is escalating in Los Angeles, California; Houston, Texas; and Miami, Florida.
> The following individuals will speak at the meeting: Delores Humphrey, F.B.I. representative; Marcus Romelo, Forensics Bureau; and Ben Ruben, Domestic Violence Bureau.

PART D

The Colon

Rule 1. Use a colon after the salutation of a formal letter.

    Examples: Major Montgomery:
                       Corporal Swanson:

Rule 2. Use a colon when indicating standard time (no colon is needed when using military time).

    Examples: Our classes begin at 8:40 A.M.
                       The robbery took place at 11:30 A.M.

Rule 3. Use a colon when introducing a formal quote.

    Example: The framers of the U.S. Constitution believed in these words: "No man shall be deprived of the concepts of ordered liberty and fundamental fairness."

Rule 4. Use a colon when introducing a list.

    Examples: A skilled officer possesses the following characteristics: dedication, commitment, and professionalism.
                       The officer seized the following items: twelve bullets, thirteen knives, and twenty semiautomatic weapons.

Exercise 1

Directions: On the blank provided, write a **C** if the comma usage is correct or an **I** if the comma usage is incorrect.

_____   1. Correctional personnel spend a lot of time, and energy maintaining order in the prison setting.

_____   2. Violent crime is on the rise in New York, California, and Florida.

_____   3. Officer Smith entered the cell and found Jones, and Abrams in a fight.

_____   4. Drug use, which is taking place in some departments, must not be tolerated.

_____   5. Trainee Williams is a responsible, intelligent student.

_____   6. The victim said, "There's the guy who took my wallet."

_____   7. On January 31, 1997, we took the law test.

_____   8. Officer Jones writes factual reports, she has won the respect of her colleagues.

_____   9. Juvenile crime, which is reaching epidemic proportions, must be prevented.

_____   10. During the 1980s, the prison population started to increase.

Score = (# correct × 10) = _____%

Exercise 2

Directions: On the blank provided, identify the following as **C** for correct, **CS** for comma splice, **F** for fragment, or **R** for run on.

_____ 1. Officer Johnson always writes factual reports, he has won the respect of his colleagues.

_____ 2. Because Corporal Murphy reviews departmental procedures, she is able to make accurate decisions.

_____ 3. You studied diligently for the report-writing exam I am pleased to inform you that you have passed.

_____ 4. Officer Ward interviewed all inmates in the cell, and he recorded statements about the incident.

_____ 5. I want to graduate from the academy, therefore I must put forth time and effort toward my studies.

_____ 6. Studied last night for the law exam.

_____ 7. The report-writing class must be interesting, every trainee is paying close attention.

_____ 8. The report-writing class must be interesting, for every trainee is paying close attention.

_____ 9. The report-writing class must be interesting every trainee is paying close attention.

_____ 10. Because every trainee is paying close attention.

Score = (# correct × 10) = _____%

Exercise 3

Directions: On the blank provided, identify the following as **C** for correct, **CS** for comma splice, **F** for fragment, or **R** for run on.

_____ 1. Although the trusty was abiding by the policies and procedures.

_____ 2. Violent crime is on the rise legislators want to hire more law enforcement and correctional officers.

_____ 3. Communication skills are important for every officer.

_____ 4. Although communication skills are important for every officer.

_____ 5. Because he communicates effectively, Officer Randolph receives respect from the inmates.

_____ 6. Officer Brown communicates effectively, she receives respect from the inmates.

_____ 7. Inmate Smith started throwing food in the cafeteria I took away his TV privileges.

_____ 8. There is always something new to learn about the job, I will try to learn a lot.

_____ 9. All officers should conduct themselves in a professional manner.

_____ 10. When an officer conducts herself in a professional manner, she will gain pride, respect, and self-esteem.

Score = (# correct × 10) = _____%

Exercise 4

Directions: On the blank provided, identify the following as **C** if the sentence contains the correct usage of the semicolon or colon or an **I** if the usage is incorrect.

_____ 1. The inmate tried to escape; however, the officer was able to stop him.

_____ 2. The inmate said; "Tomorrow I'm out of here."

_____ 3. The riot took place at 11:45 A.M. in the cafeteria.

_____ 4. Dear Lieutenant Jones:
Thank you for meeting with me.

_____ 5. A report narrative should contain these elements: who, what, when, where, why, and how.

_____ 6. The inmate has requested the following items: blankets, pillows, socks, and books.

_____ 7. Before I go home this evening; I must finish writing the report.

_____ 8. The inmate punched a hole through the wall; then he started kicking his belongings around the cell.

_____ 9. If you are not feeling well: I will work your shift.

_____ 10. The juvenile committed the burglary; therefore, she will be incarcerated.

Score = (# correct × 10) = _____%

PART E

Quotation Marks

Rules to Remember

As report writers, you are constantly taking statements; therefore, you should be familiar with the following quotation rules:

Rule 1. Commas should be placed inside quotation marks.

> **Examples:** "About five inmates punched and kicked Lewis," said Corporal Perry.
> "A white male, wearing a black T-shirt, robbed the bank," explained the witness.

Rule 2. When paraphrasing another's statement, quotation marks are not necessary.

> **Examples:** Everett said she came home from work and found the back door open.
> Inmate Oberman said he was in the gym when he heard a scream.

Rule 3. When you are quoting a word or phrase within a quotation, use single quotation marks.

> **Examples:** The juvenile said, "I walked out of the house when a guy said, 'Give me your wallet.'"
> The victim said, "I got into my car when a voice behind me said, 'Drive.'"

Rule 4. Question and exclamation marks should be placed inside quotation marks only when they are part of the quote.

> **Examples:** "Who is in charge of the Dobson case?" asked Detective Carlucci.
> "You passed the test!" cried Trainee Andrews.

Rule 5. Question and exclamation marks should be placed outside quotation marks when they are not part of the quote.

>   **Examples:**   Who said, "Interrogate the witness"?
>   I can't understand why you think my report is "sloppy"!

Rule 6. When writing a direct quote, remember the formula: (a) comma, (b) quotation marks, and (c) capital letter.

>   **Examples:**   The victim said, "That's the guy who destroyed my store."
>   The inmate said, "He punched me in my face, so I punched him back."

Exercise 1

Directions: Insert quotation marks where they are needed.

1. The chief said, Welcome to one of the finest departments in the state.

2. Drop your gun! screamed Officer Metz.

3. Did you call the crime scene unit? asked Officer Ford.

4. The clerk said, He pointed a gun at my face, and I thought he was going to kill me.

5. Review your notes on search and seizure, said Professor Newman.

6. Was it you who yelled, Fire?

7. The captain said, Recruits who are late for work will not last long in this profession.

8. Get back in line! exclaimed Sergeant Brown.

9. I recommend stress management counseling, said Officer Parlow.

10. Congratulations! said Training Adviser Richards.

Score = (# correct × 10) = _____%

PART F

The Apostrophe

Rules to Remember

Rule 1. Use the a + b approach to form the singular possessive.

    a. Write the word.

        +

    b. Add the apostrophe (')s at the end of the word.

    Example: officer + 's = officer's

    The <u>officer's</u> report is factual and complete.

    Note: The singular possessive refers to something that belongs to one person. (One report that belongs to one officer is factual and complete.)

Rule 2. Use the a + b approach to form the plural possessive.

    a. Write the word in its plural form.

        +

    b. Add an ' *after* the s.

    Example: sergeants + ' = sergeants'

    The <u>sergeants'</u> uniforms are always pressed.

    Note: The plural possessive refers to something that belongs to more than one person. (The uniforms, which belong to more than one sergeant, are always pressed.)

Rule 3. Use the apostrophe when forming contractions. The apostrophe takes the place of a missing letter.

Example: you are

you're (the apostrophe takes the place of the letter a).
You're a credit to your department.

Rule 4. Use the apostrophe to take the place of a missing number or numbers.

Examples: I arrested the suspect in '97.

The suspect was incarcerated in '97.

Exercise 1

Directions: Add the apostrophe where it is needed.

Example: (contraction)   I won't turn in my report until I proof-read it.

1. (singular possessive)   The lieutenants crime proposal was implemented last year.

2. (singular possessive)   The correctional officer documented the inmates statement.

3. (contraction)   If you are prepared, you should do well on the state exam.

4. (contraction)   The juvenile couldnt know about the crime, so he must be lying to us.

5. (plural possessive)   The officers training helped them succeed at their jobs.

6. (plural possessive)   The victims testimonies were shocking to the jurors.

7. (contraction)   You shouldnt allow stress to dominate your emotions.

8. (singular possessive)   The captains speech to the new recruits was sincere.

9. (singular possessive)   The juveniles handgun is on the table.

10. (singular possessive)   Trainee Wilsons efforts proved to be worthwhile.

Score = (# correct × 10) = _____%

Posttest

Directions: On the blank before the number, write the letter of the correct word(s) for the following sentences.

_____ 1. _____ report is on the captain's desk? _____ Officer Brown's report.
   a. Whose, It's   b. Who's, Its'
   c. Whose, Its   d. Who's, Its

_____ 2. I _____ you to seek the _____ of a skilled law enforcement officer.
   a. advice, advice   b. advise, advise
   c. advise, advice   d. advice, advise

_____ 3. _____ did the major appoint as his assistant? _____ wants to know?
   a. Whom, Who   b. Who, Whom
   c. Who, Who   d. Whom, Whom

_____ 4. The victim gave his _____ to the defense attorney who has a pleasant _____.
   a. deposition, deposition   b. disposition, deposition
   c. disposition, disposition   d. deposition, disposition

_____ 5. The habitual offender is not a _____ witness because he lacks the impressive _____ that most jurors find _____.
   a. credible, creditables, credible
   b. creditable, credibles, creditable
   c. credible, credentials, creditable
   d. credible, credentials, credential

_____ 6. While he was conducting a _____ search, the officer observed Smith climbing _____ the open window.
   a. through, threw   b. through, thorough
   c. thorough, thorough   d. thorough, through

_____ 7. A professional law enforcement officer must be _____ at _____ to the challenging conditions of the job.
   a. adept, adapting   b. adopt, adapting
   c. adept, adopting   d. adapt, adepting

_____ 8. _____ going over _____ to retrieve _____ weapons.
   a. There, their, they're   b. Their, there, their
   c. They're, there, their   d. They're, there, they're

_____ 9. When he confronted the fugitive, the _____ officer believed he was in _____ danger.
   a. eminent, eminent   b. imminent, eminent
   c. imminent, imminent   d. eminent, imminent

_____ 10. Although the officer's belt was _____ he did not
_____ his gun. This would have resulted in a
_____ of departmental property.
   a. loose, lose, lose   b. lose, loose, loss
   c. loose, lose, loss   d. lost, loose, loss

_____ 11. Officer Jones was _____ for a promotion. However,
his writing is _____ and he participated in
_____ conduct; therefore, he was not promoted.
   a. eligible, illegible, elicit   b. eligible, illegible, illicit
   c. illegible, eligible, illicit d. eligible, eligible, illicit

Directions: On the blank provided, place an A if the sentence
is written in the active voice or a B if the sentence is written in
passive voice.

_____ 12. The officer found the victim's body near the side of
the road.

_____ 13. The defendant confessed to killing the elderly man.

_____ 14. The officer received an award for his outstanding
service to the community.

_____ 15. The evidence was taken to the crime lab by the
officer.

Directions: On the blank provided before the number, write the
letter that identifies the correct form of the verb.

_____ 16. Neither of the inmates _____ been granted parole.
   a. have
   b. has
   c. both a and b are correct
   d. both a and b are incorrect

_____ 17. Several of the captains _____ going to the
conference next week.
   a. is
   b. are
   c. both a and b are correct
   d. both a and b are incorrect

_____ 18. All of the officers _____ their writing skills.
   a. have improved
   b. has improved
   c. both a and b are correct
   d. both a and b are incorrect

_____ 19. Either of the trainees _____ capable of achieving
a high score on the exam.
a. is
b. are
c. both a and b are correct
d. both a and b are incorrect

_____ 20. Neither of the officers _____ ready to retire from
the law enforcement field.
a. are
b. is
c. both a and b are correct
d. both a and b are incorrect

Directions: On the blank provided before the number, write the
letter that identifies the word that is spelled correctly.

_____ 21. The officer confiscated _____ from the defendant's bedroom.
a. barbiturates   b. barbituates
c. babituates

_____ 22. The criminal justice _____ offers many challenging opportunities.
a. proffesion   b. profesion
c. profession

_____ 23. I have a _____ for your arrest.
a. warrent   b. warrant
c. warant

_____ 24. The _____ spoke at the meeting.
a. leiutenant   b. lieutenant
c. lieutenent

_____ 25. All officers should conduct themselves in a
_____ manner.
a. curteous   b. courteous
c. corteous

Directions: On the blank provided, identify the punctuation as
A (correct) or B (incorrect).

_____ 26. On December 17, 1996, investigators discovered the
gruesome evidence.

_____ 27. When the four juveniles started fighting, the officer
called for assistance.

_____ 28. You studied diligently for the exam; I am pleased to
inform you that you passed.

_____ 29. Police reports should be written in a clear concise,
and accurate manner.

_____ 30. The following elements should be included in the
narrative: who, what, when, where, why, and how.

_____ 31. Because I want to graduate from the academy, I
must put forth time and effort toward my studies.

Directions: On the blank provided before the number, write the
letter that identifies the correct set of pronouns for the following
sentences.

_____ 32. The detectives questioned _____ and _____
about the murder.
a. him, her   b. him, she
c. he, she   d. him, I

_____ 33. _____ and _____ graduated first in our class
at the academy.
a. She, him   b. He, I
c. She, me   d. He, me

_____ 34. Officer Gleason and _____ visited _____ in
the hospital.
a. me, him   b. I, him
c. I, he   d. me, he

_____ 35. The major had to choose between _____ and
_____.
a. he, she   b. him, I
c. he, her   d. him, me

Directions: On the blank provided, place an A to indicate a fragment, a B to indicate a run on, a C to indicate a comma splice,
or a D to indicate a complete sentence.

_____ 36. Violent crime is on the rise legislators want to hire
more law enforcement officers.

_____ 37. Officer Taylor interviewed all witnesses, and he
recorded their statements in his report.

_____ 38. The report report-writing class must be interesting,
every trainee is paying close attention.

_____ 39. Officer Jones always writes factual reports, he has
won the respect of his colleagues.

_____ 40. Seized the narcotics.

Directions: On the blank provided, place the letter that identifies
the subject in the following sentences.

_____ 41. Because he consistently studied, Trainee Jones
graduated with honors from the academy.
a. academy   b. Trainee Jones
c. consistently studied   d. graduated

_____ 42. In order to intimidate their victims, offenders will
often use threats, obscenities, and weapons.
a. offenders   b. threats, obscenities, and weapons
c. victims   d. intimidate

_____ 43. Inmate Smith spoke to Corporal Murphy about the
incident, which took place in the gymnasium.
a. incident   b. Corporal Murphy
c. gymnasium   d. Inmate Smith

Directions: On the blank provided, place the letter that identifies
the type of the underlined words in the following sentences.

_____ 44. I'm going to the major's retirement party.
a. contraction, plural possessive
b. contraction, singular possessive
c. contraction, singular
d. contraction, plural

_____ 45. The officer documented the victims' statements.
a. plural, plural possessive
b. plural, singular possessive
c. singular possessive, plural possessive
d. singular, plural possessive

Directions: Each sentence contains one error. On the blank
provided, identify the error by its letter as follows: A (grammar),
B (punctuation), C (spelling), or D (capitalization).

_____ 46. The jury foreperson said, "We find the defendant
guilty of the charges.

_____ 47. At 2300 hours, I searched the suspect's van and
seized six knifes, which were on the front seat.

_____ 48. When the alarm went off at 3:15 A.M., neither of the
intruders were ready for a confrontation with the
police officers.

Directions: On the blank provided, place an A if the sentence is
written in first person. Place a B if the sentence is written in the
third person.

_____ 49. I searched the interior of the suspect's car.

_____ 50. This officer searched the interior of the
suspect's car.

Directions: On the blank provided before the number, write the
letter of the correct response.

_____ 51. Reports should be written in the past tense. Which
sentence is appropriate for past tense writing?
a. I questions the juvenile.
b. I questioned the juvenile.

_____ 52. Identify the correct pronouns for this sentence:
He spoke with _____ and _____ about the
incident.
a. him and me   b. he and I

_____ 53. Is this sentence written in the active or passive
voice? I ordered the inmate to step out of the cell.
a. active   b. passive

_____ 54. Is this sentence written in the active or passive
voice? The cell was searched by me.
a. active   b. passive

_____ 55. Is this sentence written in the active or passive
voice? I wrote the report.
a. active   b. passive

_____ 56. Which word is spelled correctly?
a. patroled   b. patrolled

_____ 57. Which word is spelled correctly?
a. received   b. recieved

_____ 58. Which word is spelled correctly?
a. believed   b. beleived

_____ 59. Is the punctuation usage correct or incorrect? I questioned the inmate. I escorted him to confinement.
a. correct   b. incorrect

_____ 60. Is the punctuation usage correct or incorrect?
Crime is on the rise; citizens want to feel protected.
a. correct   b. incorrect

_____ 61. Is the punctuation usage correct or incorrect?
Crime is on the rise, citizens want to feel protected.
a. correct   b. incorrect

_____ 62. Identify the correct word for the sentence. My
weapon is over _____.
a. there   b. their
c. they're

_____ 63. Identify the correct word for the sentence. I _____
the stolen merchandise.
a. seized   b. ceased

_____ 64. Identify the correct word for the sentence. _____
is my report?
a. Were   b. Where
c. Wear

_____ 65. Is the sentence written in the first- or third-person
style? I handcuffed the inmate.
a. first-person style b. third-person style

_____ 66. Is the sentence written in the first- or third-person
style? This officer responded to a back-up call.
a. first-person style b. third-person style

_____ 67. Is the sentence written in the first- or third-person style? This unit transported the inmate.
a. first-person style   b. third-person style

_____ 68. Is the sentence a fact or an opinion? The inmate was hostile.
a. fact   b. opinion

_____ 69. Is the sentence a fact or an opinion? The inmate yelled, "Don't touch me!"
a. fact   b. opinion

_____ 70. Is the sentence a fact or an opinion? The woman left the store without paying for the merchandise.
a. fact   b. opinion

_____ 71. Is the sentence a fact or an opinion? The officer writes good reports.
a. fact   b. opinion

Directions: On the blank provided, write A for grammar error, B for spelling error, or C for punctuation error.

_____ 72. I recieved a call about a fire.

_____ 73. He tells me he did not see anything.

_____ 74. The inmate said, "He pointed a gun at my back."

_____ 75. The inmate raked the leafs in the compound.

Directions: On the blank provided before the number, write the letter that identifies the correct word to complete the sentence.

_____ 76. He is the officer _____ I recommend.
a. who   b. whom

_____ 77. The guard dog used _____ strength to stop the burglar.
a. its   b. it's

_____ 78. Each of the juveniles _____ been incarcerated.
a. has   b. have

_____ 79. The officer was traveling _____ on the highway.
a. North   b. north

_____ 80. The sergeant had to choose between _____.
a. her and I   b. her and me

_____ 81. The robbery _____ at 11 P.M.
a. occurred   b. occured

_____ 82. The officer confiscated drug _____ from the car.
a. paraphernalia   b. paraphernelia

_____ 83. The inmate said, "_____ out of my cell."
a. Get   b. get

_____ 84. The attorney has an interesting _____ about the
case.
    a. perspective   b. prospective

_____ 85. The fight was _____ three males.
    a. among   b. between

_____ 86. Neither of the officers _____ called in sick.
    a. has   b. have

_____ 87. The juveniles brought _____ weapons to school.
    a. their   b. there   c. they're

_____ 88. The sergeant said, "_____ with the investigation."
    a. Proceed   b. Precede

_____ 89. Crime is on the rise _____ we must come up
with solutions.
    a. ; therefore,   b. , therefore;

_____ 90. Officer Garner is an _____ representative.
    a. intelligent professional
    b. intelligent, professional

_____ 91. I was _____ the area at 1600 hours.
    a. patroling   b. patrolling

_____ 92. _____ is handling the Nelson case?
    a. Who   b. Whom

_____ 93. The annual report approved by _____ is on your
desk.
    a. Chief Brown   b. chief Brown

_____ 94. The jury members believed the _____ testimony.
    a. officer's   b. officers

_____ 95. _____ a credit to the law enforcement profession.
    a. Your   b. You're

_____ 96. Both of the officers _____ been promoted.
    a. has   b. have

_____ 97. _____ is your report.
    a. Here   b. Hear

_____ 98. I _____ a commendation letter from a citizen.
    a. recieved   b. received

_____ 99. The juvenile fled the scene.
    a. active   b. passive

_____ 100. The scene was fled by the juvenile.
    a. active   b. passive

Score = (# correct × 1) = _____%

Glossary of Writing, Grammar, and Word Usage Rules

Active Voice	A sentence in which the subject performs the action.
Example:	Active: <u>I wrote</u> the ticket. Passive: The ticket <u>was written by me</u>.
Adjective	A word that describes a noun or pronoun.
Example:	The <u>skilled</u> officer conducted a <u>lawful</u> search.
Adverb	A word that describes a verb. Adverbs commonly end in *ly*.
Example:	He hesitated <u>momentarily</u>.
Among	Relates to <u>three or more</u> persons or things.
Example:	The fight was <u>among</u> three juveniles.
Apostrophe (')	Used in the following ways: a. Forms the singular possessive case (officer's uniform) b. Forms the plural possessive case (officers' uniforms) c. Forms contractions (you're) d. Takes the place of missing numbers ('92, '93)
Article	A type of adjective. The words <u>a</u>, <u>an</u>, and <u>the</u> are articles.
Examples:	<u>An</u> inmate is afforded many rights. <u>A</u> fight took place in the gym. <u>The</u> captain held a meeting.
Between	Relates to <u>two</u> persons or things.
Example:	The decision will be <u>between</u> the two detectives.
Chronological Order	Record of facts and events in a logical, ordered sequence.
Examples:	I was dispatched to 1053 Creeks Cove. I spoke with J. Young about the incident. I arrested J. Young for aggravated battery.

Clause
A clause is a group of words with a subject and a verb. Clauses are broken down into two categories:

a. <u>Dependent clause</u>: A group of words with a subject and a verb that cannot stand alone.

Example:
When I approached the defendant's car.

b. <u>Independent clause</u>: A group of words with a subject and a verb that can stand alone as a complete sentence.

Example:
I approached the defendant's car.

Colon (:)
Used in the following ways:

a. To introduce a list
b. To indicate standard time
c. After the salutation of a formal letter

Example:
The following elements should be included in the narrative: who, what, when, where, why, and how.

Comma (,)
Punctuation mark that indicates a break or pause in the sentence.

Examples:
I wrote the report, but I did not sign it.
I studied diligently, and I graduated from the academy.

Comma Splice
An error that occurs when the writer incorrectly joins two complete, independent sentences with a comma.

Examples:
I saw the defendant run a red light, I gave him a ticket. Inmate Smith started screaming, I asked him to stop.

Conjunctive Adverb
An adverb that is used to connect two independent clauses.
A <u>semicolon</u> (;) should come <u>before</u> the conjunctive adverb, and a comma (,) should come after the conjunctive adverb.

Example:
The suspect started to run; <u>however</u>, the officer was able to stop him.

Contraction
A shortened version of a longer word or words. An apostrophe (') is used to take the place of the missing letter.

Examples:
<u>You're</u> a credit to the law enforcement profession.
<u>Didn't</u> you hear the loud crash?

Coordinating Conjunctions
Words (*and, but, or, nor, for, yet*) used to join sentences or sentence parts.

Examples:	I will study for the test, <u>and</u> I will be prepared. I arrested the suspect, <u>and</u> I drove him to the station.
Exclamation Mark (!)	Used to illustrate anger or emotion.
Examples:	Help! He stole my purse! Duck! He's got a gun!
First-Person Reporting	A style recommended for writing reports. Writers should use <u>I</u> or <u>we</u> to identify themselves on reports.
Examples:	<u>I</u> questioned her about the arson. <u>We</u> drove the suspect to the jail. <u>I</u> arrested him for burglary.
Fragment	An incomplete thought occurring because it is a group of words that lacks either a subject or a verb.
Examples:	That she heard screaming. (incorrect) She heard screaming. (correct)
Homophones	A word that has a similar sound as another word but is spelled differently and has a different meaning.
Examples:	I <u>accept</u> the promotion. (accept) Everyone was at roll call <u>except</u> Officer Connors. (except)
Interjection	A part of speech that expresses emotion.
Examples:	Stop! Police! Put your hands up!
Misplaced Phrase	A phrase that gives an altered meaning to the sentence because it does not describe what it is intended to describe.
Examples:	I saw ten pounds of marijuana walking down Ocean Avenue. The officer ate a turkey sandwich on the bench with mustard.
Nonrestrictive Phrase	A phrase that is not important to the overall meaning of the sentence.
Example:	Captain Kowalski, <u>one of our fine administrators</u>, is retiring after 25 years of service.
Noun	A word that identifies a person, place, thing, or idea.
Examples:	badge (concrete) Judge Williams (proper) officer (common) team (collective) honesty (abstract)

Objective Pronoun	A pronoun that is used as the <u>object</u> of a sentence.
Examples:	We questioned <u>him</u> and <u>her</u>. They asked <u>us</u> for permission to leave.
Parts of Speech	The way each word in a sentence functions.
Examples:	a. Noun: officer, badge, jury, inmate b. Pronoun: I, you, he, she, it, we, us, them c. Adjective: blue, red, loud, soft d. Verb: ran, sat, studied, talked e. Adverb: (commonly ends in *ly*) slowly, quickly, momentarily f. Conjunction: and, but, or, nor, for, yet, so g. Interjection: Wow! Hey! No! h. Preposition: (linking words) like, on, near, from
Passive Voice	A sentence in which the verb expresses an action performed on the subject or when the subject is the result of the action.
Examples:	(passive) The suspect was transported to the jail <u>by me</u>. (active) <u>I</u> transported the suspect to the jail. (passive) The car was hit <u>by lightning</u>. (active) <u>Lightning</u> hit the car.
Past Tense	Form of a verb that indicates a past time. Often reports are written in the past tense format because the event has already occurred.
Examples:	I <u>arrested</u> the suspect. I <u>questioned</u> the witness. I <u>told</u> the defendant to stop.
Period (.)	Used to end a complete sentence or statement.
Examples:	I was dispatched to Rosemary Road<u>.</u> I saw the suspect weave in and out of traffic<u>.</u>
Preposition	The preposition is used to <u>link</u> sentence parts.
Examples:	I left my report <u>on</u> the desk. I questioned the suspect <u>about</u> the homicide.
Pronoun	Used as a substitute for a noun.
Examples:	<u>She</u> is the author of the published manual. <u>He</u> is going to a conference next week.
Punctuation Marks	Marks used to make the meaning of a sentence clear to a reader: a. Apostrophe (') b. Colon (:) c. Comma (,)

d. Exclamation mark (!)
e. Period (.)
f. Question mark (?)
g. Quotation marks (" " or ' ')
h. Semicolon (;)

Quotation Marks	Most commonly used to introduce a quote.
	a. Double quotation marks (" ")
Examples:	Inmate Youngblood said, "He stepped on my foot, so I punched his face."
	Taylor (witness) said, "I saw the white car spin out of control and hit the red car."
	b. Single quotation marks (' '): Used to identify a quote within a quote.
Examples:	The reporter said, "Ms. Jimenez told officer Jarvis, 'I saw a man running from the scene.' "
	Judge Stanis said, "I will accept the defendant's statement, 'I am not guilty.' "
Run-on Sentence	Sentence that allows two sentences to run together without proper punctuation and/or conjunction.
Example:	Prisons across the country are overcrowded inmates are being released early.
Semicolon (;)	Punctuation mark used in the following ways:
	a. To join two independent sentences.
	b. Before a conjunctive adverb when joining two independent statements.
Examples:	The officer arrested Smith; he transported Smith to the station.
	Agf. Morales stopped a speeding car; however, he gave the driver only a warning.
Sentence	Group of words containing a subject and a verb. A sentence expresses a complete thought.
Examples:	I conducted a search of the suspect's home.
	I frisked the inmate for contraband.
Subject	Used to identify who or what performs the action in a sentence.
	Answers the following questions:
	a. What is the sentence about?
	b. Whom is the sentence about?
Examples:	<u>Inmate Smith</u> went to prison for his crime. (Who went?)
	<u>Officer Vargas</u> was honored at the meeting. (Who was honored?)

Subjective Pronoun	A pronoun that acts as the subject of a sentence.
Examples:	<u>She</u> called the police. <u>He</u> told me to watch the inmate.
Third-Person Reporting	Identifying the writer of a report as "this writer," "this officer," or "this unit." The third-person reporting style is not recommended for reports.
Verb	A word that identifies action or being. A verb is essential to form a complete sentence.
Examples:	He <u>pointed</u> a gun at my head. I <u>am</u> the person who arrested her.
Who	Used as a <u>subject pronoun</u> in a sentence.
Examples:	<u>Who</u> called the meeting? <u>Who</u> wrote the arrest report?
Whom	Used as an <u>objective pronoun</u> in a sentence.
Examples:	<u>Whom</u> did the chief interview for the position? <u>Whom</u> did the witness identify in the lineup?
Who's	The contraction of <u>who is</u>.
Examples:	<u>Who's</u> going to the law enforcement banquet? <u>Who's</u> replacing Chief Wilson?
Whose	Word that shows ownership.
Examples:	<u>Whose</u> report is on my desk? <u>Whose</u> car is at the garage?

Recommended Reading

The following resources are highly recommended for further reading:

Dillingham, William; Martin, Edwin; and Watkins, Floyd. *Practical English Handbook.* Boston: Houghton Mifflin Company, 2000.

Ehrlich, Eugene. *Oxford American Dictionary.* New York: Oxford University Press, 1980.

FDLE: Law Enforcement Guidelines, Basic Recruit Training Curriculum, 2006.

Goodman, Debbie J. *Enforcing Ethics.* Upper Saddle River, N.J.: Prentice Hall, 1998.

Merriam-Webster's Collegiate Dictionary. Springfield, Mass.: Merriam-Webster, Inc., 2003.

Index